MY WIFE TOLD ME TO GO TO THERAPY

A Guide for Men on How to Love The 21st-Century Woman

Stacy Lund, LCSW, CCTP,
& Stephanie Sisson, LCSW

Jacket art: by Rony Dhar

Registration Number: TXu 2-475-083
ISBN: 979-8-8959037-4-2

The views and opinions expressed in this manuscript are our own and do not reflect the views of any affiliated organization. *The case studies and stories in this text are shared with proper permissions, and identifying details, including names, have been altered to protect privacy.*

Ordering Information:
Interested in ordering 10 or more copies?
Email us at
Twinperspectivesinfo@gmail.com
for our current discount schedule.

Sign up for our free monthly newsletter:
www.twinperspectivesllc.com

Thank you to the men who inspire.
To the men who model what real partnership looks like—you are living proof that love can be both strong and tender. You're the ones who crack open a beer while changing a diaper, who don't think twice about picking up tampons, and who willingly sit through *Bridgerton* because you know that *is* the kind of sexy that matters.

Thank you to the women.
To every woman who has sat on my couch, sharing your stories of frustration, heartache, and hope—you are the reason this book exists. You gave me the courage to tell men what women truly want and the conviction to remind you that you deserve nothing less.

Thank you to our readers.
You are the brave ones—the ones willing to reflect, learn, and grow. This book is for you.

Thank you to my best friend and sister, Stephanie.
Thanks for agreeing to take this crazy journey with me without hesitation.

And to my husband.
Thank you for being my partner, my teammate, and my constant reminder that love is a journey of growth.

– Stacy

Table of Contents

Prologue

I am sitting on a cold, hard metal bench at the park, watching my five-year-old daughter spin on the merry-go-round. *This* merry-go-round is a modern plastic version of the old metal third-degree-burn-waiting-to-happen kind many of us grew up with. It is the first day of January, and the kids in our school district are on winter break for a few more days. It is a sunny but chilly 25-degree day. This is the type of cold that sneaks up on you, seeps into your bones, and before you know it, you cannot feel your face. The radiant sunshine is deceptive because I still need to wear every piece of outside gear I own to stay warm today. I am all bundled up with my coat, hat, gloves, scarf, and boots. I live in Salt Lake City (SLC) with my husband and our three children. Although I have lived here most of my life, I still cannot get used to the cold. I *hate* the cold. Nothing will sour my mood faster than the cold. At this moment, I'm doing my best to concentrate on the scene unfolding in front of me with the most positive attitude I can muster. A cousin of mine once said that "having kids means never being comfortable again." He is about ten years older and, at the time, had five young children with a set of triplets in the mix. I have often thought of this statement over the last decade, which is when my parenting journey began. Being uncomfortable is not an uncommon feeling thus far in my parenting experience. Before I was a child, I would never voluntarily spend time outside in 25-degree weather. I do not ski, sled, ice skate, snowboard, or snowshoe, so there is no logical reason for me to be outside right now. On top of the cold weather, Utahns deal with air pollution and inversion during the winter months. The mountains create a perfect "soup bowl" full of polluted air in which the toxins linger over the valley and cannot escape. It is a difficult balance to ensure your kids are getting enough exercise and vitamin D and not too much poisonous air.

My daughter feels this is perfectly acceptable weather to ride her bike in. I have decided that children must have an uncanny ability to turn off their senses in the name of play. There is a visible amount of snow on the mountain bench, but there is none in the valley thus far. This is not great for tourism to the local ski resorts, and it's definitely not great for the dwindling water levels of the Great Salt Lake. Each year, the wait for snow feels longer. My daughter is wearing outdoor gear, which is pink and purple from head to toe. She's *also* wearing a Spiderman bike helmet.

A hand-me-down from her older brother. She has asked several times for a new helmet, but I've been trying to extend the life of this one to avoid the cost of a new one as long as possible. In the springtime, we will pick out a new helmet that she likes with a unicorn or mermaid on it, something pink, purple, sparkly, and jeweled.

When we first arrived at the park today, a little boy asked her to join him on the merry-go-round. This big, bright red, plastic monstrosity has little indentations that serve as a place for the children to sit. As they spin slowly around, several of the little boys begin talking enthusiastically about Spiderman. I can see the excitement and acceptance of this particular topic on several little faces. An older boy says something I don't catch. Another boy responds, "Girls can like boy things." He seems proud as this is also the boy who eagerly asked her to join their play. I think, "*Hell yeah, girls can like boy things!*" I feel proud, too. A rare moment of parenting victory!

This is short-lived as another thought occurs to me: I have two boys of my own. My husband and I are attempting to raise them to be kind, strong, vulnerable, motivated, passionate, self-aware, and creative men. As a toddler, my son Dylan loved the color pink until kindergarten, when his classmates insisted he wasn't allowed to. I attempted to tell him he could like any color in the world and that pink was a great color. I even told him how pink had started as a masculine color. In

Victorian times, it was a color used in many boys' nurseries, birth announcements, and clothing. This was to no avail. He now loves the socially accepted color red.

I love muscles. I love the smell of my husband's deodorant. It smells like wood shavings and some kind of citrus. I love that he keeps his hair short and shaves his facial hair away. I've always had a thing for the athletic type or a guy in uniform. All three of my first serious relationships were with men who served in the Marine Corps. I also love vintage fashion, pedicures, cooking, antiques, and home renovation reality TV. These things fall neatly into what is expected of me as an American woman. This isn't necessarily a problem. It becomes a problem when I begin to over-identify with these things—if I use these traits to control others, to believe I am superior, and put everyone else in a box labeled inferior. Human beings categorize and judge as a way to make sense of our world. Unfortunately, this continues to cause problems in the form of stereotypes, stigma, oppression, etc., which results in divisiveness. We are living in an extremely divisive time. As Fred Dust (2020), author of *Making Conversation,* states, "We have moved from 'I'm right and you are wrong' to 'I'm right, you're wrong, I hate you, and you're lying.'" This rigidity can easily bleed into our personal relationships. Couples get lost in who is right and who is wrong when this isn't even what matters. It is time we all work toward equality despite our differences and accept that we are all human.

We are witnessing a gender and sexuality cultural change. 7% of Americans identify as gay, bisexual, or transgender (Brown, 2023). More of us are questioning gender identity and roles. Women are increasingly choosing to be single or file for divorce in order to increase career success as well as freedom (Emamzadeh, 2022). Some couples are in an "open relationship." Polyamory is a common term but still widely misunderstood. I have recently heard the term *Toxic Monogamy*, which I feel is, ironically, hypocritical. Any relationship can be toxic regardless of the category it fits into. Ten million Americans a year experience domestic violence (National Coalition Against Domestic Violence, n.d.). 42-53% of marriages end in divorce, with the U.S. having the 13th highest divorce rate in the world (World Population Review, n.d.). All of this data seems to suggest we still have not figured out how to couple effectively, and attempting to put everyone in a blue or pink box just isn't working for our current culture.

This book is going to examine how all this change, as well as rigidity, is impacting us within our intimate relationships. We will examine the history of male and female roles in America and how it continues to repeat itself. Why is this important? Remember the all-too-famous quote, "Those who do not learn from history are bound to repeat it"? Understanding the failures and pitfalls of the past will help motivate you to change as well as decide what you want for the future. This book will help you navigate our ever-changing roles to create loving and HEALTHY relationships. My generation has lived through a pandemic, a war, a recession, the women's movement, the loss of women's reproductive rights, climate change, "fake news," parenting with technology *everywhere*, and a sexual/gender revolution. Due to easy access to information, many of us are aware of the cracks in the foundations of many of our institutions. However, this book is not an attempt to put people in boxes labeled good or bad. It is a guidebook for change and growth. It is a road map for finding a healthier, happier you.

INTRODUCTION:

The 21st-Century American Man (by Stacy)

"How long has it been since you last cried?" I ask. I sit with a long pause, and then Brian answers, "Years." I know he is taking his time to speak in order to avoid letting his grief escape and take over. I am not surprised by this answer. I expected it, but I feel a squeezing around my heart when it comes. I am reminded of my mentor's words at the Veterans Administration (VA): "Hide the tissues until they are covered in snot. You want to give them a chance to get it all out." Ben was one of my favorite mentors—a clinical social worker who had served in Operation Iraqi Freedom and Operation Enduring Freedom (OIF/OEF) and continues to serve today. We spent nine months together on the Inpatient Psychiatric Unit (IPU) of the Salt Lake City VA. Before entering graduate school, I was working with aging adults. I have worked with several veterans on hospice services. I've never had the heart to hide the tissues. Brian doesn't take one, anyway. He uses his sleeve and sniffles loudly. This vulnerability is beautiful and scary at the same time. I wonder if I have pushed too far too quickly, as we have just begun working together. I begin to weave a web of safety in this emotional and physical space we share. It is my ethical and moral duty to ensure he leaves feeling grounded and stable.

It's a picturesque summer morning in my small, quaint office located in downtown Salt Lake City. This particular office has recently been renovated and stylishly decorated. I love this building. It's old and has character. You can quickly see it is at least a hundred years old due to the exposed brick and single-pane iron-framed windows. One of the windowpanes is cracked, and a small piece of glass is missing. I'm already planning to find the duct tape to cover the hole when I get a chance.

Brian is a thirty-two-year-old army veteran who has come to see me to help manage his symptoms of PTSD. He has a mostly athletic build, a little thin, dark eyes, and a full beard and head of chocolate-brown hair. He has many tattoos spread around the visible parts of his body. I'm wondering if he is wearing facial hair to hide his age or to stray from the typical clean-cut style the military requires. During OIF/OEF, American service members were encouraged to grow beards as this was a sign of masculinity and strength. The typical clean-cut appearance required of US soldiers didn't quite cut it in the Middle East. Brian, like many servicemen with combat experience, has seen too much. This changes a person. He is more nihilistic now and stuck, at times, in existential dread. Sometimes his words reflect the sense of hopelessness he feels. Brian has a young daughter and is newly married to his second wife. He recognizes how his trauma has been impacting his relationships, which is a large part of why he is sitting across from me on a beautiful Saturday morning. I imagine there are many other places he'd rather be, but he has decided to walk through the hellish memories of the past with me.

Gender Inequality Applies to Men, Too!

Gender inequality impacts everyone—men and women alike. Today, American men face challenges in education, economics, emotional well-being, social connections, and domestic roles. Women, on the other hand, are excelling academically but still encounter barriers to earnings and career advancement (Gender Gap: This Is the State of Work for Women in 2024, 2024).

For decades, conversations about gender inequality have rightly focused on empowering women. However, it's time to broaden the discussion and examine how men are negatively affected by gender norms and expectations as well. This book doesn't advocate for a matriarchal society or pitting one gender against another. Instead, it's about fostering true equality—where support for one group doesn't come at the expense of another.

Initially, this book aimed to help men become better partners. But as the research unfolded, it became clear that many men are struggling to connect with a fuller, happier life. For instance, married men statistically live longer, enjoy better sex lives, and earn more (Why Are Men Overlooking the Benefits of Marriage? | UNews, n.d.). However, when those marriages are high-conflict, men experience lower levels of happiness and well-being, further emphasizing the importance of healthy relationships (Harvard Health, 2019).

Some may argue that a return to 20th-century gender roles is the solution—but that's neither realistic nor desirable. Women, having experienced greater opportunities, won't willingly return to an era of diminished choices. On the flip side, there's also pressure for men to abandon traditional masculinity altogether—a demand that's biologically and socially untenable.

So, what's the answer? Equality and equity must begin at home. When relationships are rooted in mutual respect and shared responsibility, this mindset extends to the workplace and broader society. Men will feel empowered to seek better work–life balance, just as women have fought to do, without fear of being penalized. A more balanced approach to emotional and domestic labor—like sharing the mental load and household responsibilities—will benefit everyone.

The shifting dynamics have left many men questioning their roles. Women can now financially support themselves, and as Richard V. Reeves of the Brookings Institution points out in *Of Boys and Men*, some women increasingly view male partners as just "another mouth to feed." He explains, *"The dramatic rebalancing of power relations between men and women over the last few decades has rendered old modes of masculinity, especially as family breadwinner, obsolete. But nothing has yet replaced them"* (Reeves, R. 2022).

The goal isn't to strip men of their identity or their strengths. It's to redefine masculinity in a way that aligns with today's reality—giving men the tools to thrive in every area of life, from work to relationships, without compromising their sense of self. Men in America are facing a crisis—one that is quietly wreaking havoc on their lives and our culture. Despite being a smaller percentage of the population, men account for alarmingly higher rates of addiction, incarceration, unemployment, and suicide (USAFacts, 2024).

These statistics are not just numbers; they tell the story of a deep cultural issue—a loss of purpose and place for many men.

The suicide rate for men is staggering; in 2022, men were 3.85 times more likely to die by suicide than women (Suicide Statistics, 2024). As of July 6, 2024, 93.2% of the U.S. prison population was male, compared to just 6.8% female (BOP Statistics: Inmate Gender, n.d.). Men over 20 also face slightly higher unemployment rates than women (3.5% vs. 3.2% over the past two years), with unemployed men ages 25-54 steadily increasing in number (US Bureau of Statistics, 2024). According to a 2016 Brookings Institution report, many of these men lack the skills or education to stay competitive in today's workforce. Disturbingly, these men are not compensating by taking on more childcare or household responsibilities. Instead, they're disengaging, with more time spent watching TV than their employed counterparts (Wessel, 2016).

In the fall of 2022, undergraduate enrollment included 6.1 million men, significantly fewer than the 8.3 million women (NCES, n.d.).

Men are also less likely to graduate on time; in 2014, only 41% of men completed college within four years, compared to 51% of women (NSCRC, n.d.).

Substance use is another area of concern. Men are more likely to misuse alcohol, prescription drugs, and illicit substances, leading to higher rates of addiction, overdoses, and emergency room visits than women (NIH, 2022). In 2020,

17.7% of men aged 18 and older had a substance use disorder, compared to 13.2% of women (SAMHSA, n.d.).

These statistics paint a bleak picture but point to a path forward. If men begin to engage with the emotional and social aspects of their lives—if they embrace the opportunity to connect more deeply—they will no longer live on the surface. With this engagement comes purpose, belonging, and, ultimately, better mental health.

Glennon Doyle encapsulates the experience of
American men in her book, *Untamed*:
"A fifteen-year-old school shooter who killed three
classmates, one of whom was a girl who had
rejected his advances.
Members of a lacrosse team
charged with gang rape.
A college boy killed in a hazing incident.
A middle school gay boy who hung himself
because of bullying.
A thirty-five-year-old decorated veteran who had
just 'succumbed to PTSD.'
Oh my god. This is what it looks like for boys to
try to comply with our culture's direction. They
are not allowed to be whole either. Boys are in
cages, too" (Doyle, 2020).

The system isn't working—not for men, not for women, not for anyone. To address this crisis, we need to move beyond outdated cultural expectations and build a society where men feel free to live whole, connected, and purposeful lives. The stakes are too high to ignore.

Who We Are and Why We Wrote This Book:

Stacy Lund is The Clinical Director of a trauma clinic in Salt Lake City, Utah. She is a Licensed Clinical Social Worker (LCSW), a Certified Clinical Trauma Professional (CCTP), a trained yoga teacher, and a certified Eye Movement and Desensitization (EMDR) clinician.

Stephanie Sisson is a Licensed Clinical Social Worker practicing in Beloit, Wisconsin. She specializes in Grief and Trauma and is EMDR-trained. She has practiced in three states, including Utah, New Mexico, and Wisconsin.

Stacy and Stephanie are identical twin sisters who were raised in Salt Lake City, Utah. They both earned their undergraduate and graduate degrees at the University of Utah College of Social Work.

As social workers, one of our core ethics is social justice. We eat, live, and breathe anything that will help us accomplish social justice in this crazy world. We decided to write this book in hopes of helping individuals as well as couples find more fulfilling relationships. We assume you have picked up this book because your relationship is in trouble, and we believe we can help you save it. This book will also encourage you to see a mental health clinician regularly because we believe you will benefit from a skilled guide through this journey. You may also consider a couple's counselor or sex therapist to help foster mutual love and respect. Mutual love and respect must be present within a relationship for it to thrive and be sustainable.

Before we begin, let's talk about defensiveness and shame. I feel it is vital we discuss defensiveness and shame before going any deeper. If we don't, you probably won't make it through the book before chucking it across the room. We will be talking about hard things—things you won't want to hear. Defensiveness may show up, so I'm going to prepare you ahead of time so you know what to do when it does.

Defensiveness and shame show up in our arguments and cause major damage as well as stalemates. Let's call it the *Big D*. The Big D has been described to me thousands of times by hundreds of clients. When they sit and talk about a recent disagreement, I'm waiting for the Big D to rear its ugly head. It's typically only a matter of time. Defensiveness is a defense mechanism that often creeps up in order to avoid feeling shame or guilt. Shame is the most uncomfortable emotion we feel as human beings. No wonder we avoid it like the plague! However, shame is just a teacher. It is a normal human emotion we all feel. It reminds us to not make the same mistake again. If we didn't feel ashamed, we wouldn't have morals. We would navigate the world selfishly and wouldn't care who we hurt. That would be a scary world. Shame is only problematic when it becomes toxic shame. Toxic shame is when we let our mistakes define our value. "I accidentally hit the car next to me at the grocery store. I'm such an idiot." You get the point. When shame shows up, just remember it's trying to teach you something. Learn from it, change your behavior, and move forward.

Dr. John and Julie Gottman are world-renowned clinical psychologists who have been studying and working with couples for over 50 years. They created the Seattle Love Lab, where they have studied over 3,000 couples (The Gottman Institute, 2019). If you end up in couples counseling, chances are your therapist will be using their techniques to help repair the issues in your relationship. The Gottmans list defensiveness as one of the Four Horsemen of the Apocalypse. The other three horsemen are contempt, criticism, and stonewalling (The Gottman Institute, 2024). We will discuss the Four Horsemen in further chapters. For now, just remember defensiveness is bad. Defensiveness can look like talking in circles, trying to prove who is right or wrong. It can also look like manipulation by changing the subject or bringing up all your partner's faults or past mistakes to displace blame. It may show up in my favorite way. *I'm being sarcastic here.* Perhaps you acknowledge you are wrong and continue with an explanation, such as, "You are right. I'm the worst partner in the world. I don't know why you are with me." This display of low self-esteem is actually hiding defensiveness. This forces your partner to comfort you or reassure you they won't leave. And then, guess what? Nothing changes.

When you have a disagreement with your partner, try to hear what the need is and what your part is in any hurt that may have occurred. You may need to request a time-out to calm down in order to think about things from a logical place. When we argue heatedly, we activate our brains' survival response network and cannot engage our executive functioning skills, which include logic, reasoning, and the ability to consider the consequences of our actions (McKay et al., 2023). Make sure you verbalize to your partner you need some time to calm down and think. If you storm off, she may feel abandoned. One more thing: Give her a time frame of when you would like to talk again about the issue, so she doesn't feel as if you are sweeping it under the rug.

When you are able to be calm, you can ask these three questions, which will be a good place to start:

1. What does my partner need? Connection, reassurance, safety, validation?
2. What am I doing that isn't working in this relationship?

3. Is there something I need to apologize for and work to repair?

My Wife Told Me to Go to Therapy is a title Stephanie and I laughed about when spit-balling ideas for the book. We were discussing how often men come with this as their primary reason when asked why they are seeking therapy. They aren't always sure what the problem is. They just know they are on thin ice and need to "get help." So, if you are reading this book, chances are you have a partner who has demanded you go to therapy "or else."

Although you are probably aware of the difficulties within the relationship, you may not agree that they actually merit a need for therapy. Common questions that can come up when therapy is mentioned are "Isn't therapy for couples who are going to divorce/break up?" and "What do I even talk about?" You may be afraid to ask your partner for details as to what exactly to go to therapy for because this may result in another epic argument or the statement from your partner that "you should already know what the problem is because I've told you so many times!" So, you will just book the appointment, show up, and have the therapist tell you what to do, am I right? Or perhaps you have been in therapy for years for self-improvement, career goals, etc., but try as you might, you still end up having the same three arguments with your partner over and over again. Maybe you have always felt you needed therapy but never took the steps to make it happen, and this ultimatum is the perfect excuse to finally do the work.

Regardless of your previous experience with therapy, or lack thereof, I personally do not feel you should go to therapy unless you have some desire to do so.

Therapy can be useful for anyone *if* they are open and willing to examine themselves and the things in their lives that are not serving them.

I think of it like brushing your teeth or drinking enough water throughout the day. Talk therapy can be a large part of your mental health hygiene. In American culture, we like to think of the brain and body as separate, but they are intricately connected. I could go into a lot of detail about that here, but that information is for another book. However, we will briefly discuss this in a later chapter when we discuss stress management. Many of us go to the gym, see the dentist every six months, and get the occasional massage. Unfortunately, Americans don't always value mental health, which, ironically, can have a major effect on physical health. So, if for no other reason, you *could* go to therapy for your physical well-being.

If you decide to take the leap and see a therapist, finding a clinician you feel comfortable with is important. This comfort will grow with time, allowing for more vulnerability and healing. A good therapist will push you out of your comfort zone and sometimes even tell you things you may not want to hear. They will hold you accountable and be your cheerleader, all in the name of mental health. So, pick wisly, and don't be afraid to do a few first sessions with a handful of different clinicians. Working with a clinician you like will go a very long way. You do not have to be best friends, but you do have to respect their opinions and feel safe with them. This book will help you be prepared to enter therapy and get the most out of your time there.

That said, going to therapy once a week will not be enough to fix the problems within your relationship. A huge part of therapy is applying what you learn during the weeks and hours between sessions. So, get ready to work on and off the couch.

There are many amazing therapists in the field. Clinicians who specialize in relationships, trauma, sexual intimacy, effective communication, etc. Clinicians typically have an area of focus with specialized training and expertise in their area. This means some clinicians will lack a deep understanding of the true cause of difficulties within intimate relationships as well as the depths of its impact. How do I know this? As a clinician, I took courses in gender studies, sex therapy, couples counseling, communication, and attachment—but I still didn't understand.

I thought I knew the basics of managing relationship conflicts. Unfortunately, there was a piece of information missing. I believed I understood all the reasons we hurt each other and how to heal, but I was ignorant of something fundamental. I saw the problems and the solutions, but I wlked right past the machine that was continuously pumping these issues out on a conveyor belt. I have spent the majority of my career learning how to heal trauma. This is my passion. I believe trauma is the cause of all the suffering in this world. Throughout the years, I have spent countless hours reviewing just about every aspect of my clients' childhoods, their attachment styles, and the way they love and were loved. I have discussed generational patterns within family systems that affect my clients today. In this journey to understand, I began to notice common patterns. These patterns were reflected within my clients' relationships with childhood caregivers and the way they relate to their relationships as adults. Any book on trauma will discuss these patterns in great detail. I have been trained to notice these patterns. I know them like the back of my hand. I can tell you that how your mother handled money affects your financial values. I can tell you why you don't like it when someone uses a certain word when angry with you or why you feel numb to emotions. Although my education, research, and collected qualitative data shed light on my clients' issues, it was not the whole picture. It has only been through my ten-plus years of speaking with (mostly) women, as well as being a woman in a heterosexual relationship, that I began to piece it together.

So, why, after so much knowledge and research has been gathered on coupling, are we still shooting in the dark? This is because, in many relationships, the source of the problem is *invisible*. Yes, you read that correctly. The problem is invisible. Also, most of the population has been trained to ignore and minimize the problem. Many grunt, groan, and roll their eyes when this issue is addressed, assuming they have heard it all before. This response is hardwired within us to avoid change in the system. This is the part where I tell you I am going to challenge you. I am going to hold you accountable. I am going to tell you things you do not want to hear. I am going to flip your worldview upside down. You will have to look at beliefs you may not realize you have and actively work to let them go. You may have to start questioning the way things were done within your family of origin and the way things were done within society as a whole. There may be times you must question your spiritual beliefs and what it means to be a man, a father, son, brother, or friend. This is not easy, but it is absolutely worth it. Discomfort is a sign of change. You can and will learn to use discomfort to your advantage, as well as learn how to navigate difficult interactions with others in a more effective way. If you want to spend your life being the best version of yourself as well as having healthy, fulfilling relationships, this book is for you.

It is common knowledge that all couples have disagreements that fall into one or several of these categories: sex, money, labor, spirituality, parenting, etc. Typically, we laugh about this and accept it as unchangeable. This is because the approaches typically taken are ineffective. Some of us end up in couples counseling, talking to clergy, friends, or family for advice, reading self-help books, finding ways to avoid disagreements, or arguing and making up (repeatedly) to eventually end the relationship. There is a common saying among couple's counselors: Most couples enter couples therapy five years too late. I believe, with the help of my coauthor and many clinical geniuses who have gone before me, this book can help you enter therapy and begin to repair the damage of these never-ending arguments. I believe in you and your ability to change. Human beings are resilient, with the ability to learn from the mistakes of past generations. I am not saying you will never argue again or that you will never hurt your partner again, but it will become the exception, not the rule. Arguments will be an opportunity to create a deeper, healthier relationship. So, if you are going to argue, do it right. Get the most out of your conflict and create something amazing in the process.

Disclaimer: If your relationship involves abuse, addiction, or severe mental illness, this book alone will not be sufficient. It is important to mention couples therapy is not recommended in cases of domestic violence (Huffine, 1999). While this book offers valuable tools and resources, these challenges require a strong network of support. Take what is helpful from these pages but also seek out your village—your trusted support system—to guide you through.

Although this book was written for a cisgender heterosexual male audience, this book may be relevant or helpful for LGBTQ couples as well. I hope LGBTQ couples will find something of value within these pages. We would love feedback for further research and understanding.

We also recognize that, as two cisgender white females, we cannot fully understand the experience of members of minority groups who have experienced discrimination and oppression. We understand how this may affect these individuals' relationships in ways not addressed within this text.

You may spend six months in therapy learning coping skills, how to communicate in a healthier way, what your personal love language is, as well as your attachment style, etc., only to continue having the same arguments with your partner. Within my clinical career, I have seen this dynamic play out more times than I can count—this pattern of personal growth and healing with an inevitable roadblock.

We are writing this book because we are burnt out from having the same one-sided conversation. The *female* side of the conversation. Don't get us wrong, we adore our clients, but it takes two to tango. We can only get so far by focusing on her and her alone. Once we have exhausted what she has control over, we look at codependency, childhood trauma, boundaries, and personal values. My clients heal and grow and work hard to do so. If they have a partner who refuses to grow alongside them, this is when the relationship can feel stuck. This sometimes leads to a breakup with a difficult grieving process included. We refer our clients to couples therapy, hoping they find a clinician who validates their experiences and supports growth and equality in their relationship.

This recommendation may end in my client giving the dreaded therapy ultimatum. Assuming one partner can go to therapy to fix all the issues is as ridiculous as giving your partner an ultimatum to go to therapy. Couples need to work as a team to find common ground, make compromises, learn from past hurts, and change behaviors that damage the relationship. This means work for both people in the relationship.

As previously stated, our clients typically report arguments are often focused on finances, sexual intimacy, in-laws, housework, parenting, or emotional availability. Again, let me say these issues are part of a much larger problem. The above issues are the acorns on the branches of a mighty tree. You want these problems gone? Then you have to dig up the whole damn tree. You must accept this tree is toxic and not serving you. It will take back-breaking work with little recognition from your partner (at first). You may have people in your life telling you they think you are weak for destroying the tree. They may tell you this makes you less of a man. There may be an internal voice whispering, "I have a right to have this tree in my yard, damn it!" This is all part of the lie you and many before you have been told. So, stop believing the lie. The lie isn't serving you or your partner.

The therapy ultimatum is one many men are receiving in our changing American culture. This is not a new ultimatum but one that appears to be increasing. Dr. Deryl Goldenberg, a clinical psychologist who has focused on male psychology as well as couples, explains many men believe therapy is for the weak or severely mentally ill. It's only when their relationships are at risk (particularly their sexual relationship) that they begin to open up to the idea of going to therapy (Goldenberg, 2017). If you have received this ultimatum, try to view it as the next adventure in the book of life. Abraham Maslow, a renowned American psychologist, believed all human beings have a need for self-actualization or, in simplest terms, a need to meet their full potential (Sullivan, 2016). Rigidity or refusing to change sabotages self-actualization. Your partner has indicated there is a need for change; we are creatures of habit, which means we do not always love change. We are also adaptable and resilient. If I didn't believe this and had not witnessed it many times, I would not be in my profession.

One of the top reasons people end up in therapy is because of the relationships in their lives. This could involve relationship challenges with a partner, boss, parent, child, or others. Many people assume that relationships fail primarily due to poor communication.

Although this does have some merit, it is typically a small piece of the relationship trouble puzzle. Communication is another false lead and will not give you a full view of the problem. If you are feeling completely lost because you have been trying to work on your relationship but end up in the "same argument, different day," this book is for you. This book will help you walk into therapy better prepared. I have worked with men as well as alongside male clinicians. I have researched and studied men's issues, but this has only further deepened my belief we are missing something vital as clinicians. So, how can men entering therapy because of an ultimatum hope to get the help they need when they have been told they just need to "work on communication"? You have to stop believing this and other pop psychology garbage first. This is where I tell you it's time to choose the red or blue pill. The red pill is ignorance, and the blue pill is truth. I hope you choose the blue pill.

Okay, now that we've got *that* out of the way, I want to briefly go over what will be covered in this book. In Chapter 2, we will briefly discuss the issues causing problems in most American relationships. Chapters 2 and 3 will discuss how the problem shows up in our daily lives as men and women, respectively. Chapter 4 will cover emotions, and Chapter 5 will discuss how chronic stress impacts us. Chapter 6 is the toolbox. This is the nuts and bolts of how to use the knowledge provided in the previous chapters to move toward a healthier and happier relationship. We have included a chapter on sex (Chapter 10)! Of course, sex is important and shows up eventually as a source of issues within any relationship in one way or another. In Chapter 7, we give you exercises and tools to begin taking on a fair amount of emotional labor and mental load. Chapter 8 covers boundaries, how to set them, and why they are important in our relationships. Chapter 9 covers our favorite frameworks and approaches to parenting. If you don't have children and think this isn't relevant, you may be tempted to skip this chapter. I believe you may still learn something important, and we encourage you to avoid the temptation to skip ahead. Finally, we will provide further resources in the appendix because this book is meant to be short and sweet. We could not cover everything within this book, and let's face it, no one would read a thousand-page book on relationships.

CHAPTER 1:

Put The Toilet Seat Down! (by Stephanie)

In order to explain the concepts within this chapter, I would like you to imagine a scenario. Let us just pretend for a moment that you and your best guy friend decide to open a small auto shop business together. You pool your money and rent a space in a premium location. Neither one of you has experience in business or are trained mechanics, but you both love cars and know a lot about the various makes and models. There is no discussion beforehand about who will be "the boss" and little discussion about which tasks will be assigned to each of you At first, things run quite smoothly as you both just pour yourself into the business and enjoy this new adventure together. You find that as important financial decisions come up, you tend to assert yourself and take them on without much thought. You like your friend, but you feel you are generally more business-minded, so you are, therefore, better equipped to handle this side of things.

You both work long hours in the shop every day, but you spend a lot of time in the office ordering and tracking parts, managing the finances, and marketing the business. Your friend, on the other hand, spends much of his time cleaning up after the mechanics and organizing the shop space so tools and parts are easy to find. He also starts cleaning and maintaining the bathroom and break room himself and other necessary janitorial tasks because you cannot afford to hire someone for that. He deals with payments at the cash register and any angry customers. He even handles the mechanics when they have a need or complaint. He pays attention to when someone is going to be taking time off or who is out sick and lets you know.

After a few weeks pass, your friend starts to complain regularly about how much he must do around the shop every day and states that he feels it is unfair that he does all the physical labor while you are almost always found in the office sitting at the computer or on the phone. He asks if you can help more with some of his usual tasks, so it feels fairer. Not wanting to lose your friend and business partner, you apologize and tell him you will try to help him more. However, on the rare occasions when you do sweep the shop floor, deal with a customer, or take out the trash, you make sure to point this out to your friend because you feel you are doing him a favor and that these tasks are generally beneath you. You very rarely give him praise when he does these same tasks because you feel that this is his job and expected of him.

You share a little about finances with your friend, and he must come to you when he wants to purchase anything new for the shop because you do the ordering and the inventory. You, however, purchase things as you see fit and do not ask his input or for permission. He points out this double standard, but you tell him this is only because you are better at managing the finances, and he can come to you anytime to request an order or ask to see the books. What you do not admit is that when he asks for something you feel is unreasonable, you guilt or shame him about it and treat him like a kid asking for additional allowance. You show him the bookkeeping when he asks, but this annoys you because you feel he should trust you, and you let him know it. After a while, your friend stops asking for anything other than the usual needed supplies, and he stops asking to see the books because he knows it will just irritate you.

You have the same arguments many times over many months, perhaps even years. You never understand why he is so upset, and honestly, you feel he is just overreacting or being difficult. Over time, your friend stops bringing complaints to you and seems to generally turn his focus to his work. You feel glad about this and think that perhaps he has finally accepted that this is the best way to run the business. One day, which seems completely "out of the blue," however, he quits, demands his share of the business equity, and leaves you to run the business alone.

Now, let's compare this scenario to a marriage or other monogamous relationship that is just starting out. Like the two friends, we have two people who are starting a new adventure together, and both are usually excited and eager to get started. Just like our business owners, neither are experts on marriage or monogamy, and there is typically little to no discussion about who will do what tasks within the shared household.

Types of Labor

In our business partner scenario, the tasks within the shop were divided based on your perception of who was most capable of the task, and the rest fell on your friend by default. In typical American households, however, tasks are often given based on gender and are largely done by women, to be more specific. According to a Psychology Today article published in 2021, "It's well-documented that in the majority of U.S. families, women do more of the household chores compared to men, even when both spouses work full-time jobs."

Another important aspect of workloads when considering couples is "the mental load." These are the tasks that take regular and ongoing mental effort to keep things running smoothly. A Harvard doctoral student, Allison Daminger, divided the mental load process into four parts: Anticipate, Identify, Decide, and Monitor. Examples of each would be: **Anticipating** that soccer practice usually runs late, so dinner will need to be prepped the night or morning before. **Identifying** that you are low on laundry soap, so you plan to pick some up on the way home from work tonight. **Deciding** to take your mother and mother-in-law to brunch for Mother's Day this year and calling ahead to make reservations. **Monitoring** your child's chores and giving allowance based on chores completed each week. Just like household chores, the burden of the mental load is typically invisible to those who do not carry it and is almost completely borne by women.

Finally, there is emotional labor. This is the emotional work required to maintain relationships. It can be anything from letting your partner vent to you, being respectful during arguments, giving praise when they help you, or keeping track of upcoming social events you both attend. Women complete 2.6 times more emotional work than men do, according to a 2018 study by United Nations Women, a division of the United Nations that works for gender equality and female empowerment.

Now that we understand that in the typical American home, women do most of the household chores, even when they work full-time, carry most of the mental load, and are expected to bear the brunt of the emotional load as well, is there any wonder that your female partner often seems angry, frustrated, or just plain exhausted?

Resentment and Detachment

The typical trajectory that we see as psychotherapists is that when one person in a relationship feels the workload is consistently unfair, they first try to approach their partner with these feelings. Unfortunately, what we also often see is that these feelings are met with defensiveness, dismissal, or worse, verbal and or physical aggression. These reactions to conflict relay the message to your partner that "it's not safe to approach me about anything I don't agree with you on." This, in turn, shuts your partner down, and they are less likely to approach you in the future. This may feel like problems of the past are forgotten or let go of, but please do not be fooled. What really begins to happen is *emotional detachment*. Emotional detachment is the lack of emotional intimacy in a relationship. The problem with emotional detachment is that, over time, it can turn into something that is even more dangerous to your relationship: *resentment.*

According to Verywellmind.com, "Resentment involves feelings of anger or bitterness, over a slight injustice or a major incident." Why is resentment so dangerous to your relationship? It's because it is like a snowball rolling downhill, becoming a bigger and bigger problem. An article on Marriage.com states, "A partner harboring resentment may exhibit passive-aggressive behavior, making subtle negative remarks or displaying a generally negative attitude. The presence of resentment contributes to a toxic emotional environment, pushing the couple further apart."

If you look back, you can recall that we saw this detachment-turned-resentment scenario with our business partners. You had dismissed your friend's complaints, became irritable or defensive, and even used guilt or shame to deflect. Eventually, he stopped coming to you with needs or complaints, and he began to detach from you and, most importantly, the dream of running a business together. This is when we hear clients say things like, "I can't deal with it anymore," or "I'm just not happy," and sometimes even, "I want a divorce."

Before you get discouraged, remember that the very point of this book is to prevent the failure of your relationship. We must look at what you are doing wrong to understand how to get it right. The next chapter will explore and bust the myths about males in our culture and in relationships. It will challenge outdated views, and it will encourage a growth mindset.

NOTES :

CHAPTER 2:

What's In Your Man Box? (by Stacy)

"Nothing is so strong as gentleness; nothing so gentle as real strength."
– Francis de Sales

There are many myths, beliefs, and stereotypes in American culture and around the world about what it means to be "a real man." These gender stereotypes are sometimes referred to as the "Man Box." MensLine Australia is a free, government-funded support program for men struggling with issues within their relationships. MensLine describes the Man Box as being an unhealthy stereotype with societal pressure of conformity. Some of the elements within the Man Box are centuries old and reinforce female gender stereotypes. There is no doubt that men have biological differences from women. Richard V. Reeves with The Brookings Institute explains men differ mostly in aggression, risk, and sex, and "environment and culture weigh heavily too. It is not nature *or* nurture. It is nature *and* nurture" (Reeves, 2022). We will explore the Man Box within this chapter and how its components impact women. Before we dive in, it is important to briefly discuss a few talking points explaining how the Man Box shows up in our daily lives.

You may hold the belief that housework is for women because your mother, aunt, or grandmother always did it. They cooked the meals and washed and put away the dishes while the men in the family sat around the table or living room, talking about sports or politics or even watching a game on television. The expectations of what it means to be a man may have been taught to you from a pulpit during Sunday sermons spoken by a religious leader. Christian-based faiths use the term *Complementarianism*, which is a theological term used to describe the roles and responsibilities of women and men within a marriage.

Complementarianism suggests women and men are equal but have complementary roles for optimal spiritual well-being. This term has also been interpreted differently within many evangelical communities, which explains women should be subordinate to men, specifically their husbands (Barr, 2021).

Other definitions include a belief that only men should hold positions of authority within the church and women should support this leadership role through submission (theopedia.com, n.d.). The Danvers Statement, written by evangelical leaders in 1987, defended the position of the necessity of male authority and specified gender roles within a marriage. Bible verses were interpreted to support this position, including Ephesians 5:21-33, Colossians 3:18-19, Titus 2:3-5, 1 Peter 3:1-7 (*CBMW*, 2023, July 10). In 2020, the Public Religion Research Institute (PRRI) reported that 70% of Americans identify as Christian (PRRI, 2020). So, chances are, even if you do not identify as Christian, you have been around plenty of people who do, which may have impacted your worldview on gender roles.

In my home state of Utah, 56% of the population belongs to The Church of Jesus Christ of Latter-day Saints (LDS), which is also a Christian-based faith (Seariac, 2020). The religious text of the LDS church does not specifically state that a woman's role is to stay at home, but church leaders have spoken about the LDS position. In 1979, President Spencer W. Kimbal, a religious leader of the LDS church, wrote:

"Some women, because of circumstances beyond their control, must work. We understand that. We understand further that as families are raised, the talents God has given you and blessed you with can often be put to effective use in additional service to mankind. Do not, however, make the mistake of being drawn off into secondary tasks which will cause the neglect of your eternal assignments such as giving birth to and rearing the spirit children of our Father in Heaven. Pray carefully over all your decisions" (Wright, 2022).

Despite these words being written four decades ago, the women I see in my practice who were born and raised within the LDS faith or other Christian-based religious organizations often report guilt around working outside the home. This guilt and toxic shame increase if they have children. I have not had one male client confess feelings of being a bad father because he is not a homemaker.

It's common to see women on the television screen, social media, magazines, etc., engaging in domestic activities. It's a little harder to find images of men engaged in domestic duties outside of mowing the lawn. This paradigm of women inside the home and men outside the home has been a standard in American homes for many generations. Before the Industrial Revolution, Americans lived in farming and agricultural communities. Families worked on the land together and managed the household. Women took care of children and did physically demanding chores such as carrying water, grinding grain, churning butter, and making food and clothing. They were viewed as equal members of the household.

When machines were invented to mass produce goods, men began leaving the home to work in buildings or factories (*The role of Women in the Industrial Revolution | Tsongas Industrial History Center*. (n.d.). There was a period when families worked together as a team in factories. However, due to harsh and dangerous working conditions, women and children began to return to work primarily in the home. This is when men began to be viewed as "good providers" (*History of the Organization of Work: Industrial Revolution, Labor Unions & Automation*, 1999b). Perhaps none of the men in your family announced, "The women in the family will do all of the domestic labor!" but through the power of observation, you have held this belief your entire life. If, for example, your father refused to take his shoes off and tracked mud through the house, which always led to a fight with your mother screaming about her newly mopped floors, you might have the idea a mopped floor is not a big deal. This minimizes and devalues the effort it took your mother to mop the floor. Maybe your father responded by telling her she was overreacting or that he had worked a hard, long day and that she needed to get off his back. This would subconsciously relay the message that the work your father did outside the home was more important. Maybe it was always your mother who booked the dentist and doctor appointments and took time off work to take you. This would again reinforce the idea that the work your mother was doing outside the home wasn't as important as the work your father did, even if your mother was a doctor and your father sold software. These seemingly innocent interactions and behaviors pave the road for how children will navigate their relationships as adults. You may not even know you are helping perpetuate this belief in your relationships. You might proudly think of yourself as a feminist, but feminism needs to exist in the home as well as when you interact with your female friends.

If you have a strong subconscious belief that domestic labor falls mostly in the pink (woman) box, you will tend to believe other such stereotypes. These include, "Housework isn't my job; she's making a big deal over nothing; she's just being a neat freak." You may have such thoughts when you try to help, "I'm just helping her" or "She's so lucky I'm willing to do this; my dad never folded towels," followed by a desire for a standing ovation from your partner when you help with household chores. Unfortunately, these ideas will only fuel your resistance and increase the probability of the help you *do* provide being subpar. If you are going to create a healthy relationship, however, you will need to first notice this resistance and challenge it. You will have to give up the defensiveness and shame when exploring the Man Box.

Again, this book isn't to force you into a box labeled "JERK." If, while reading this, you felt some guilt or shame, that's a normal and understandable response. Guilt and shame serve an important purpose. These are the emotions whose job is to teach us morality as well as how to be better people. When we refuse to learn, get defensive, or shut down, this can create toxic shame. This will come as no surprise: Toxic shame is *bad*, and it gets you nowhere. Perhaps you have made mistakes in your relationships in the past. You don't have a time machine to go back and change that, but you can change your future behaviors. It may be six months before your partner begins to trust the changes you are making, but remember, actions speak louder than words. Keep doing the actions to show her you care. Don't expect forgiveness or gratitude for some time. If your partner has been completing most of the emotional labor for years, full repair may not happen for years. You do not get to put a timeframe on someone's forgiveness, but my guess is she's worth the wait.

Now that we have shame and guilt out of the way, let's begin excavating the Man Box. I have provided an imaginary scenario below to help you better understand the components of the Man Box. The below analogies aren't perfect and are an oversimplification of relationship difficulties, so try not to get caught up in the details.

Imagine you and your spouse are stranded on a desert island with a few other survivors. You are very lucky because, among the survivors, there is a doctor, an engineer, an avid outdoorsman, and a bodybuilder/dietitian. Your wife happens to be a nurse. You are a software engineer.

Once everyone has accepted the fact that it may be several weeks before a search and rescue team arrives, everyone gets to work. The engineer helps plan and build shelters with the help of the bodybuilder and outdoorsman. The outdoorsman, doctor, and your wife find food and clean water. Every night, the group builds a large fire for warmth and to hopefully catch the notice of a passing plane or ship.

Over several weeks, your wife helps the doctor attend to bug bites, sunburns, and other hazards of living in the elements. You have food, shelter, clean water, and a loving partner to share your hut, but you still feel as if something is missing. No, it's not Wi-Fi! You attend the nightly fireside gatherings but have little to talk about as the conversation is typically focused on the next day's to-do list. You feel you have little in common with these people and don't quite fit in.

Despite your wife attempting to involve you in the conversation, you feel you are just too different and give up trying to engage in the discussion. You have always been a man of few words, even around your buddies back home. Outside of sports, technology, and beer, you have little to say, and since the island has none of these things, you find yourself speaking a few words at most throughout the day. At one point, you tried to help and make nice by sharing some berries you found, but the *know-it-all outdoorsman* informed you they were poisonous.

Other attempts to build shelter and gather water and food feel like they are well in hand. You feel like you would just get in the way. Most of your time is spent attempting to catch fish. Occasionally, you are successful. You share your catch with your wife but figure the rest of the group can get their own fish. If they weren't so busy exploring the island, they could have their own fish dinners. Your wife appears ungrateful and embarrassed by the fish offerings, which leads to arguments and outbursts. She tells you she thinks you are selfish and demands you help out more. She doesn't believe spending all day catching fish for the two of you is enough. After this outburst, your wife begins spending more time with the other survivors and tells you she will catch her own fish in the future. Ironically, she's very good at it.

As for sex, it's been non-existent since landing on the island. At first, you assume the stress is too much and she will come around eventually. Occasionally, you complain and argue that sex will help lower her stress levels. She mumbles something about you helping more. Weeks later, she storms out of your shared hut, screaming, "You never sweep the floor even though I've asked you a million times!" You tried to sweep the hut once, but it wasn't done to her standards, so again, you gave up. You think the people on this island are perfectionists, overachievers, and over-emotional. From then on, your wife bunks with two other survivors.

Once rescued and back in the real world, you are quickly served divorce papers. One more important piece of information I didn't mention: You were the only man on the island. All the other survivors were women.

This scenario embodies many roles men fall into within our culture, as well as how these roles segregate them from their female counterparts. The women in the group know how to communicate, build relationships, and organize, plan, and execute their plans to ensure the survival of the group. This *is* emotional labor. The male in this situation focused on his singular duty of keeping himself and his spouse fed, which, in turn, pushed him out of the group as he was seen as selfish and lazy. He wasn't enjoying the benefits of the relationships that were created through shared emotional labor. This is why he felt unfulfilled and that something was missing. Emotional labor is the glue that keeps our social systems functioning.

In our scenario, the man's self-focused behavior was embarrassing for his wife, as everyone else was thinking about the group. It's hard for women to understand why emotional labor seems so impossible, invisible, and unimportant to their male partners. This is because it has been taught, observed, and reinforced to women since birth. As I mentioned at the beginning of the book, these gender differences can destroy a relationship. Men may be behind in emotional labor, but I fully believe they can learn. We will give you strategies for learning and catching up in Chapter 7.

I recognize women play a role in this as well. We, as women, need to let go of perfectionism and allow our partners to make mistakes to learn. We need to ask for help with specifics and not expect our partners to be mind-readers. However, there are *many* books out there that have already been written informing women of this, so I'm not going to spend much time on this issue. My focus is mostly on the male side of the coin.

I know what you are thinking: "If I had been in this scenario, I would have gone into problem-solving mode and delegated jobs. I would have helped!" To this, I say, I bet you absolutely would have helped. However, this scenario was purposely written to explain what happens day to day for many couples on a smaller scale. I hope you can honestly say you did not align much with the man in our analogies, but remember, there are many men in our culture who probably do. Either way, I think the analogy is relevant.

Now, let's use another example you might better relate to. Your wife asks you to pick up cupcakes for your kid's classroom. This is a contribution to the group that maintains the relationship between your child, his classmates, his teacher, and you as the parents. I promise you the classroom teacher appreciates your support. Teachers are barely hanging onto their sanity. Between large classroom sizes, low pay, and low funding, it's amazing anyone does this job. The children also appreciate your cupcake offering. Kids. Love. Cupcakes. Well, mostly the frosting, but I digress. The flavors you pick are vanilla and chocolate, which ensure each child will have a cupcake they like. Some children don't like chocolate. *I know*, I can't understand this either, but there it is!

If, for some reason, you forget the cupcakes, this is another job added to your partner's plate. More emotional labor on top of the Mt. Everest-sized pile she is already navigating. She may have to drop everything, run to the store, and then apologize profusely to the teacher for *her* scattered brain. If these slip-ups continue to happen, she will begin to trust you less and stop asking for help and support with the emotional labor. WARNING! DANGER ZONE! This is a huge red flag. Once she stops asking for your help with the emotional labor, resentment will begin to grow. Sir, you are now entering the waters of breakup or mediation and divorce. So, don't forget the cupcakes, and don't expect your partner to clean up the mess when you drop the ball.

At this point, you may be thinking, "It's just some stupid cupcakes," which leads us to our next section. It's not just cupcakes. This is the proverbial squeezing the toothpaste from the middle or leaving the toilet seat up. This is way bigger than a package of cupcakes, so let's talk about why continuing to believe this and other myths is problematic. Below are nine common myths that wreak havoc in our relationships.

Myth Number One: Women are Just Better at this Stuff (i.e., Caregiving and Domestic Labor).

I currently work out several days a week with a former NFL player, who also happens to be a stay-at-home dad. We discuss how to help our kiddos manage nightmares, boredom at school, separation anxiety, etc. I have observed him on the playground with his boys, and I would say he is a more than competent caregiver. He is perfectly capable of completing emotional and domestic labor. He is also *new* to being a stay-at-home father. It has only been a few years since he exited the workforce. Currently, in the U.S., one in five stay-at-home parents are fathers. The number of stay-at-home fathers has been steadily rising since 1989 but continues to be a small part of the population (Fry, 2023). My gym mate did not have his wife telling him what to do every step of the way, so how did he figure it out if men are bad at this stuff?

The same parts of the brain utilized for memory, organization, focus, and emotional intelligence exist in the male and female brains. In the book *The Male Brain,* Dr. Louann Brizendine explains when a man becomes a father, hormones in the male brain, including testosterone, prolactin, oxytocin, and dopamine, change to create optimal bonding between father and child. She further explains that after the birth of one's child, a part of the brain called the parental instinct area is activated in the mother and father to ensure optimal bonding (The Male Brain, 2010). Richard V. Reeves discusses this in his book *Of Boys and Men*: Testosterone levels fall among men with a wife and children and drop more if they are providing childcare. "Men have an evolved neuroendocrine architecture shaped to facilitate their roles as fathers and caregivers as a key component of reproductive success" (Reeves, 2022). This seems to suggest that, on a biological level, men are also wired to be kind, caring, and compassionate caregivers.

According to Dr. Michelle Ramsey, children understand gender roles by age three, and emotional labor is learned mostly through how we were nurtured (Hartley, 2018). This means we learned through observation, mirroring, and instruction from caregivers, teachers, etc. Anyone can learn how to run a household efficiently if given the proper resources and support. This is not a female-only club. So why is emotional labor so important? Women want the home to be clean and tidy to avoid a buildup of germs, which leads to illness, and toys picked up to minimize tripping hazards. We make sure the laundry is done so you have your favorite gym shorts ready for Monday morning when you head off to pump iron. We do the grocery shopping so our kids will have their favorite snacks when they come home from school. These domestic chores are, in fact, emotional labor.

When men choose to do household chores, they tend to opt for ones that need to be done every few days, weekly, or occasionally, such as mowing the lawn or changing the oil in the car (Donner, 2020). These tasks can easily be done on their schedule (Wanshel, 2023). Although this might help alleviate some stress for your female partner, these chores do not contribute enough to balance out the division of labor in a typical American home. Some families eventually delegate the lawn mowing and garbage duty to children. So, I wonder what is left on the to-do list for the man of the house? Manning the grill and putzing around the garage?

I hear stories from clients as well as my close friends describing this imbalance. Their partners spend the day golfing, playing video games, or mountain biking while these women feel guilty attending an hour-long yoga class. I can only imagine the pile of resentment building in a household like this. In case you still need more incentive to take on more of your share of the household chores, here is what the research shows: Relationships with a high level of equality are the happiest (Gordon, 2020), and couples who share housework have more sex (Bologna, 2023). I imagine this is because women have more energy and feel supported, which is great for libido!

Another phenomenon that may explain why myth #1 is so pervasive in the American household is learned helplessness. This is a term coined by American psychologist Martin E.P. Seligman while completing a study on classical conditioning. Seligman noticed some of the dogs in his experiment were no longer trying to avoid negative stimuli (shocks) despite there being opportunities to escape. He theorized that this psychological state occurs when one has accepted a lack of control over a situation (Nolen, 2024). I can imagine if, as a child, you attempted to help your mother clean, and your father berated you for doing women's work or your mother told you it wasn't done to her standard, you may have adopted learned helplessness for housework. There may have been similar experiences within your relationship where your partner asked you to vacuum, only to go behind you and vacuum again. We will discuss strategies for managing this in Chapter 7.

Fortunately, or unfortunately, we have an unprecedented level of access to information at our fingertips. This does not support the idea that men are helpless. There are plenty of male rocket scientists, brain surgeons, and nuclear physicists to also debunk the myth that men cannot figure out how to bake cupcakes or mop a floor. Weaponized incompetence is another term used to describe a partner who is pretending they are incompetent to avoid mundane chores, which shuffles work onto others.

An article in the Huffington Post written during the pandemic states weaponized incompetence has been highlighted due to quarantine. Women were reportedly noticing weaponized incompetence more due to being confined to home with their male counterparts. The article further explains that it's a passively aggressive way of not supporting your partner and displaying a lack of respect. The article suggests weaponized incompetence is due to the belief this work is beneath oneself.

Partners may feel they are having to constantly ask for help, which doesn't lead to help and only to mistrust (Wong, 2022). There may be some tasks you cannot, for some reason (despite much effort), complete, but I believe the majority will be within your grasp. We can easily Google information online, watch cooking shows, find books on parenting, time management, and organization at our local library, and attend community classes on meal prepping and cleaning. You can discuss ways of honing your domestic labor skills with a life coach, social worker, or licensed therapist. They will most likely have information on what is available in your specific area.

As for believing these tasks are beneath you, you will actively have to challenge this belief and work toward willing vs. wanting. Be willing to help even if you don't technically want to.

If you think you don't have time to manage all this, remember these are things your partner is making time for every day. You most likely will only need to take on half of the emotional labor. This is what we are going for. Equality. No need to be Superman. Take one class at a time, read one book on parenting, and watch a cleaning hack video on YouTube during your lunch break. You will probably gain more appreciation for your partner and have more of a sense of purpose in your life. Plus, you might get more naked time. Wink, wink. However, don't expect your partner to teach you domestic skills. You will need to find out her preferences for how and when she expects things to be done. This is just another way to walk the talk of respect and care. Do not call your sister or mother for advice on domestic labor. This will only place more emotional labor and mental load onto some other poor woman's plate.

I have now given you a basic road map, but before you sign up for that bread-baking class, I want you to *again* consider the following: The underlying problem most men are unaware of is a deep-rooted belief that domestic labor is beneath them. This is because of the gender stereotype that caring, compassion, and empathy are primarily a female thing. Women scrub toilets, not men. Behaving in ways that are feminine can be viewed as being weak and not masculine, so you cannot possibly scrub the toilet, or your gender identity is at stake. I will argue that not pulling your weight at home leads to your partner changing their perspective on your masculinity. This attitude may get you points with the bros, but it won't get you anywhere near relationship bliss.

Myth Number Two:
Only Weak Men do Household Chores.

When I hear the title 'butler,' I do not picture an effeminate man. I think of Alfred, the elderly housekeeper in the Batman saga, *or* I picture a former World War I vet who now oversees the staff of a large estate. Butlers still exist today and have always held domestic duties as part of their roles within the houses they serve. These duties include cooking and cleaning (Victorian Era, 2023). Another example of men who clean and ironically don't learn until early adulthood are men in the military. When men go through basic training, *a.k.a.* boot camp, they learn how to clean. They clean their barracks to where it would be safe for you to eat off the floor. They even learn how to fold fitted sheets! Soldiers practice shining and polishing their boots, as well as learning how to iron their uniforms to perfection. If you have ever stood next to a marine in dress blues, you will agree the word girly doesn't come to mind. But believe me, to look that damn good, he spent hours making sure every inch of his uniform was in order. Soldiers regularly dismantle and clean their rifles because the military understands the importance of cleanliness and organization. You won't get far in the military if you are a slob. The Navy SEALs are probably our most elite military force and have strict requirements on cleanliness and order. Admiral William H. McRaven states in his book *Make Your Bed* that starting the day by making your bed gives you a sense of accomplishment and will help set you up for success for other tasks that need to be completed throughout the day (McRaven, 2017). This could be a simple place to start with your domesticity. If you need to wear camouflage or white satin gloves while you clean, do it!

The point here is we only view housework as women's work because our culture keeps reinforcing this view, and we continue to support it. Women spend so much time trying to find better ways to manage the home, stay thin, and be the perfect mother when they should be asking why it's all on them. Doing it all is literally impossible and will only result in burnout. Burnout, according to Emily Nagoski and Amelia Nagoski's book *Burnout*, is "emotional exhaustion, depletion of caring or empathy, and decreased sense of accomplishment" (Nagoski & Nagoski, 2020). So, if you want your wife to continue to care about you, you will need to start sharing the load and breaking the burnout cycle many women are experiencing daily.

When women have an overwhelming amount of work and responsibility, their sexual desire can be affected negatively. A recent study of 705 married female participants (with children) had lower sexual desire when housework was distributed unequally. This article seems to suggest women's perception of their male partner was that of another dependent (Parker et al., 2022b). The point is that when your partner does everything to ensure you are taken care of physically, emotionally, and mentally, this forces her into the role of being your mother. Not your wife, girlfriend, partner, lover, friend, confidant, etc. You get stuck in the role of being another child in the house to take care of.

There is nothing that will kill your sex life faster than putting your partner in the mommy role. Do you want to have sex with your mother? No, I don't think you do. Likely just as much as your wife wants to have sex with a man who she views as another child to take care of. If you do not believe me, look up the small series of books titled "porn for women." These books depict men cooking and cleaning.

Women find equality and respect sexy. Women are tired and have little energy for sex, especially if there are children in the mix. Supporting your partner with emotional labor and the mental load will create more opportunities for intimacy and connection. This is shorthand for foreplay. Your new mantra is HOUSEWORK IS SEXY. There is a term for this, which is chore play. It's a great way to create a path to desire, so pick up the mop and bucket!

Myth Number Three: Men Don't See the Mess. The Mess is Invisible!

A study conducted in 2019 examined this myth. Participants were shown a picture of a messy or tidy room with a description of whether the room was owned by a man or a woman. The male research participants responded the same as the female participants. These men were able to identify the messy rooms as well as if the rooms needed to be tidied. The study also concluded the female-occupied rooms received more criticism from study participants. This seems to suggest women are cleaner because they fear judgment from the people they live with and from society (Thébaud et al., 2019b).

In the right circumstances, men can learn to observe and attend more closely to their environments. I have had conversations with many women over the years from family, friends, and clients who report these changes in their male partners' domestic behaviors. The research also supports that men are doing more at home. Men have doubled the amount of time they spend on domestic labor since 1965 but are still behind women. Men spend an average of 2.5 hours a day on unpaid work (domestic labor) vs. women's 4 hours (Donner, 2020). Despite this move toward shared unpaid labor in the home, research suggests we are about 151 years away from equality between men and women (It's 100 Years Since US Women Got the Right to Vote, but How Has Gender Equality Changed? 2020). I believe we don't have to wait 151 years. We can make this change now, and we can start in the home. I know this because I have also experienced this change in my own relationship.

After six years of marriage, my husband and I decided to start our family. Three months later, I was pregnant with twin boys. My pregnancy was difficult, to say the least. I am not one of those lucky women who enjoy being pregnant. It was painful, exhausting, and miserable throughout most of the eight months.

Once the boys were born, life began to move fast. Eric and I got thrown into the deep end of parenting, and we had to learn to swim *fast*. There were days I could barely keep my head above water, and I know my husband felt the same. The advice you hear about "marrying your best friend" is *true*. Eric and I were the worst versions of ourselves during this time with each other. Angry, irritable, passive-aggressive, and exhausted. This was when I decided to go back to therapy. I knew I couldn't keep going on this way, living in survival mode. I had found myself behaving in ways toward my partner that I thought I had grown out of. I had been in therapy since the age of fourteen and was a trained clinician. What? The? Hell? I had been on my own mental health journey for almost twenty years, but the birth of our boys required a higher level of internal work for me to function well with all the stress.

I began seeing a clinician who was certified in EMDR, and I started unpacking my entire life. I now know part of my anger was fueled by my own expectations. I wanted my husband to just wake up every morning, see everything that needed to be done, and prioritize it. I assumed he knew how to do this.

To be fair, my husband has a level of awareness your average man may not. His mother was the primary breadwinner in his home when he was growing up. His father worked for the postal service and was home in the afternoons cooking, cleaning, and helping with homework. If my husband had not observed this difference in gender roles, I'm not sure our marriage would have made it. I have always had the expectation of having a partner who would pull half of the weight.

My mother raised five children with a less-than-optimal level of help from my father. My father worked the graveyard shift at a local bakery and would sleep during the day. He also struggled with alcohol misuse and addiction. There were periods of time when my dad was sober, but it never lasted long. Despite all of this, I would define my mother as being a feminist. This means she believes in gender equality. A few weeks ago, I told her I have always thought of her as a feminist. Her reply was, "I didn't have a choice; I had to be." My mother attended college for the first time at age 47. It was not long after her academic career began that my father and mother divorced. I suspect part of this was due to my mother accepting that my father brought more problems than solutions to her life. She believed in her ability to accomplish her goals without a man by her side and despite cultural messages about what women should be doing. I am forever grateful to her for raising me with the expectation of an equal partner. I think Eric and I both had enough feminism modeled for us in our lives, which helped us move toward equality within our relationship.

Eric has taken on many tasks typically done by women. He sets up and takes the kids to most of their medical appointments. He packs lunches and gives the boys their medications in the morning and evening. He drops the kids off each morning and picks up our daughter or the boys from school in the afternoons. He reads to the boys every night until they fall asleep and helps with laundry and cleaning. He dusts, vacuums, and mops. Eric often works in the evenings and weekends and gets up early to ensure he is getting his professional work completed. We are both juggling the tasks of keeping our family happy, healthy, and safe. I have faith in you, dear reader, because I have seen growth and healing within my own relationship. I have also had the joy of witnessing my clients' lives change because of our work together, which often involves working toward equality within their own relationships.

Myth Number Four: Men Should Always Have the Final Say In the Relationship.

This myth *again* reflects a belief that the male in the relationship holds authority over his partner. This suggests your partner doesn't have a voice, which is the exact opposite of equality. Remember, equality is what we are going for. It isn't uncommon for individuals within a relationship to have a value difference. This could be a value around what religion to raise your children in, where to live, or how to parent. A difference in values can cause turmoil within a relationship. However, healthy couples learn to prioritize finding common ground (*From Esther Perel's Blog - Letters from Esther #36: Fighting with your Partner about Values?* (n.d.)). They don't take away their partner's power to get their way. When I speak of taking away power, this often shows up within the relationship in the form of manipulation. We could also call these tactics gaslighting, psychological abuse, or emotional abuse. These are unhealthy behaviors we do to try and get what we want.

You may think these tactics are worth it because you know what's best for the relationship. Let me tell you, you are paying a huge price for the win: your partner's trust and respect. If men always have the final say, they will need to get used to speaking to an empty room. I can also say that culturally, women are putting up with these behaviors less. If you can think of situations where you were passive-aggressive, used silent treatment, or other unhealthy behaviors, this book will help. We will provide more information on how to fight fairly in Chapter 5. All couples argue at times, but we can do it with love and respect.

Myth Number Five: It's a Man's Job to Protect Women.

It's not a man's job to protect women. It's everyone's job to protect women. We live in a society where the patriarchy is alive and well. Merriam-Webster's Dictionary defines patriarchy as a society where control by men creates a disproportionate share of power ("Patriarchy," 2024). Women experience discrimination as well as oppression due to gender every day. This is more severe for women of color, with ethnic or religious diversity outside the dominant culture, as well as LGBTQ women. The world can be a dangerous place, but even more so for women. In 2011, the U.S. ranked ten on the list of the most dangerous countries for women. The factors examined within this poll were healthcare, economic resources, cultural practices, sexual violence, harassment, violence, and human trafficking ("10 Most Dangerous Countries for Women: U.S. Is No. 10, According to Thomson Reuters Foundation," 2018).

I could not confidently or safely walk through a basement parking garage alone at 3 AM. I would need to have a male companion or a group of friends, as well as pepper spray at the ready. A man my same height, weight, and ethnicity probably wouldn't think twice while he strolled through the garage to his car. He wouldn't have to think about immediately locking his car door to avoid being raped or holding his keys in his fist as a makeshift knife just in case. The patriarchy will be explained in detail in the next chapter. For now, I have an example to share to help you understand why the myth of protecting women is problematic.

A client of mine came in frustrated about the behavior of a friend. Amber was an online gamer who had a gaming channel with a successful following. She was skilled and used to dealing with trolls showing up on her channel. She knew how to create and follow through on boundaries within her gaming community. One of her closest social support networks was a group of friends she fought campaigns with in the virtual world.

One night, while playing with this group, an unknown character approached her. This player began flirting with her and asked questions about who she was. Before she could respond, her guy friend inserted himself and began threatening this hopeful suitor. Amber's husband was also in the group and knew better than to step in. My client is highly intelligent and witty and could have handled the situation with tact. She called this unwanted bravado "being white-knighted." I hadn't heard the term before, but I understood it immediately. When her friend stepped in, he sent a clear message he did not believe my client could protect herself and needed his help. He probably assumed she would feel cared about and would be flattered by this display of masculinity. However, on top of the lack of confidence in her this displayed, the threatening language he slung at the intruder was unsettling. Despite his good intentions, this unwanted behavior would eventually lead to him being kicked out of the group.

Although there may be times your partner will want you to defend her to the death, don't assume she cannot handle herself in a verbal spar. I have also heard similar scenarios playing out in the real world with higher stakes. In traffic, a man honks at another driver and gets out of the car to shout at the offending driver through the window while his partner begs him to calm down. She's terrified the other driver has a gun and, in a rage, will shoot her partner. At the bar, a guy doesn't like the way a fellow patron sized him up or checked out his partner, resulting in one man getting in the other's face. The female stands to the side, absolutely terrified her partner will get hurt or hurt the other guy to the point of landing in jail.

These types of altercations can be traumatic for a partner, even if both men come away unscathed. These macho men may save face but at the expense of their partner's sense of safety. Leave the tactical fighting to the trained women and men who have legal jurisdiction to do so. Obviously, this does not mean you should ignore a woman in need in a life-threatening situation, but don't create a life-threatening situation to save your ego. As a man in our culture, you have a level of power automatically afforded to you. As Uncle Ben tells Peter Parker, *a.k.a. Spiderman,* "With great power comes great responsibility" (Lee, 1965). So, use your power wisely.

Myth Number Six: Men Should Figure Out their Problems on their Own. Men Who Ask for Help are Weak.

Okay, I admit it. My eyes are rolling into the back of my head. I cannot tell you how many times I have encouraged a client to ask her partner to try couples therapy with this response: "He's trying to figure it out on his own," or "He said couples counseling is for couples who are going to get divorced." I'm sure this is how it feels when a patient tells a physician they have been managing their symptoms by Googling the disease. This is why the rash is now covering their entire body and why they waited to come in until it got to the point of catastrophe.

Don't get me wrong, there are amazing resources online for mental health, but you must be skilled enough to know what to look for. This approach minimizes the amount of research as well as blood, sweat, and tears clinicians shed to be members of the helping profession. Clinicians also continue to learn and utilize the best evidence-based practices to ensure the modalities they use are the most effective. This is a requirement to hold and maintain licensure. There are some things you cannot do on your own. You wouldn't expect to do an appendectomy on yourself, so why are you expecting to heal your relationship on your own? Healing is faster with a professional guide. Okay, okay, I'll get off my soapbox.

As a species, human beings have always existed in tribes. We didn't have claws, strong pelts, tusks, or super speed, yet we survived by helping each other and relaying information, such as "I drank water from that muddy puddle, and now I'm sick." Translation: Don't drink water from muddy puddles. Oogah, ooga. Asking for help is part of being human. We are wired to need human connection. Social connection helps us endure emotional pain, learn, and align with others to create social harmony. Our brains have a system within the medial prefrontal cortex that reacts automatically to foster social connection (Cook, 2013). Dr. Bruce Perry is a skilled trauma clinician, child psychiatrist, and neuroscientist who speaks about connectedness. He explains in his book *What Happened to You?* that connectedness is the ability to maintain relationships due to learned skills and the opportunities to practice these skills within relationships. Our modern culture is creating fewer of these opportunities, resulting in relationship poverty. Online platforms decrease in-person interactions and inhibit the resources of regulation, reward, and learning we obtain from interaction with others (Perry & Winfrey, 2021).

According to the Kaiser Family Foundation, Americans aged 8-18 are spending 7.5 hours a day on screens, which adds up to 114 full days a year (*Infographics - Screen Time Vs. Lean Time | DNPAO | CDC*, n.d.). Screen time can have negative effects on sleep, cardiovascular health, BMI, poor stress regulation, insulin levels, vision, mood, and empathy (Lissak, 2018). We all need opportunities to connect with others throughout our day. Everyone needs a tribe of healthy and supportive people. This is another reason emotional labor is vital for men and women. Emotional labor is a way we can easily connect socially with others in our modern world. I took a break from writing this morning to run to the store, where I purchased cards, small toys, and gift bags. Tomorrow is Valentine's Day, and I wanted to make sure my mother, husband, and children have something special to remind them how much they are loved. I texted a fellow parent at my son's school to double-check they are passing out Valentines. I don't want to send them if not needed and potentially embarrass my son. I bought them weeks ago because I didn't want to have to rush out and fight the crowds. I purchased tickets to a play for a date night with my husband next week and secured a sitter. I responded to a friend who has a son who is looking to be placed in an internship at our agency. We set up a coffee date to catch up. All these actions are fostering and growing my tribe. They may seem unnecessary, but relationships are like plants. You must feed them, or they will die.

Admiral William H. McRaven (U.S. Navy, Retired) writes, "None of us are immune from life's tragic moments. Like the small rubber boat we had in basic SEAL training, it takes a team of good people to get you to your destination in life. You cannot paddle your boat alone. Find someone to share your life with. Make as many friends as possible, and never forget that your success depends on others" (McRavern, 2017).

On the inpatient psychiatric unit (IPU) of the Salt Lake City VA, our team psychiatrist would often tell the veterans, "The secret of life is finding something you love and someone to do it with." Isolation and the risk of suicide were a correlation I quickly made during my time on the IPU. The veterans would often come into the IPU and report they had been isolated for several days before landing in the emergency department of the VA. They hadn't left their apartments or homes for several days to go to the grocery shop or see friends. Some were attempting to attend college courses or work a full-time job. Some were on 100% disability, which meant they struggled with chronic physical or emotional pain due to combat experience and could not work. Usually, veterans landed on the

IPU for substance misuse relapse, a suicide attempt, or a combination of the two. Veterans would spend days to weeks on the IPU learning how to live instead of just functioning, which meant a need for regular social connection. The staff would hold processing groups and activities and discuss ways to cope in a healthy way once leaving the unit. Guess what? We often told them to get used to asking for help and support.

One of my favorite books I have read thus far as a clinician is *On Combat*, written by Lt. Col. Dave Grossman and Loren W. Christensen. Both men have served in the military and are experts in the physiology and psychology of warfare. If you want to better understand the men and women who run toward danger (our warriors), this book is a great place to start. Col. Grossman discusses the importance of asking for support. "Pain Shared = Pain Divided, Joy Shared = Joy Multiplied" (Grossman & Christensen, 2008). We cannot avoid all pain and suffering as human beings, but we may lessen the intensity and duration by speaking with those we love and trust. This could be peers, mentors, family, friends, or a mental health professional. Col. Grossman further encourages readers to always tell their loved ones you love them and give them a hug before you leave each day. "Each day is a gift." In case you fall in the line of duty, you do not want to leave your loved ones behind with feelings of regret. "Make it a habit. It is one of the best things you can do for your family, and it is a powerful gesture for yourself. And never doubt that a warrior has strength enough to love, and courage enough to show it" (Grossman & Christensen, 2008). You, too, can create a healthy support network. We are currently in a loneliness pandemic, so chances are, there are others out there looking to do the same.

The 19th and 21st Surgeon General of the U.S., Dr. Vivek H. Murthy, explains within the 2023 Advisory that the mortality rate of social isolation is like smoking fifteen cigarettes a day and is more detrimental than obesity or physical inactivity (Murty, 2023). We all need people, and at times, we all need help. It requires vulnerability and courage to admit you are human, but you are strong enough. The people in your life who truly love you will want what is best for you. They will support you when you fall and encourage you to get back up again. They will hold you accountable when you make mistakes without expecting perfectionism. If you don't have these people, find them!

Myth Number Seven: Men's Value is Based on Sexual Prowess, Wealth, and Power.

More women are initiating divorce despite negative repercussions such as increased financial burden and resulting in a need to provide more childcare (Parker et al., 2022). In 1963, women earned 59 cents per every dollar that men earned. In 2020, women earned 77 cents per every dollar their male counterparts made. Women are catching up economically, which increases their ability to be independent, and they can choose to leave an unhappy marriage (Hann, 2023). According to an article in Forbes, 34% of marriages end due to infidelity and 31% due to conflict. One of the top reasons for conflict listed was division of labor (Bieber, 2023).

More women are choosing to stay single because they feel empowered by staying single. They can focus on school and a career, have their own space, and experience the journey of being single (DePaulo, 2018). Single women must only worry about washing their own laundry and can easily travel or enjoy hobbies. According to the Pew Research Center, the number one reason couples marry in the U.S. is for love. The sixth reason was for financial stability. Having a male partner with financial stability was important but wasn't the most important factor (Pew Research Center, 2020). Love is respect, compassion, kindness, affection, passion, and connection. None of these require power, wealth, or sexual prowess. Don't get me wrong, sex is great, but how you are in the bedroom doesn't make up for poor behavior outside of the bedroom.

Myth Number Eight: Men Should Never Express Emotion Unless it is Anger or Excitement.

The Guest House is a poem I often share with my clients who struggle with emotions. Perhaps they cannot articulate what they are feeling or are afraid of certain emotions. Americans have been taught negative emotions are *bad* and positive emotions are *good*, but emotions are more complex than good or bad. Our emotions serve as messengers. Anger is typically in response to a goal being blocked or a boundary being crossed. Sadness can be an indicator of too much change or loss, which pushes us toward asking for help. Shame is, as we have discussed earlier, a teacher that helps us learn from our mistakes. All these emotions are uncomfortable but valuable. If we attempt to shut out negative emotions, we shut out positive ones, too (*Emotional Numbness – PTSD UK*, n.d.). Take some time to read *The Guest House* from this perspective.

The Guest House

This being human is a guest house.
Every morning a new arrival. A joy, a depression,
a meanness,
some momentary awareness comes
as an unexpected visitor.
Welcome and entertain them all!
Even if they're a crowd of sorrows,

who violently sweep your house
empty of its furniture,
Still, treat each guest honorably.
He may be clearing you out
for some new delight.

The dark thought, the shame, the malice, meet them at the door laughing, and invite them in.

Be grateful for whoever comes because each has been sent as a guide from beyond.

–Jalaluddin Rumi (translated by Coleman Barks) (Scottish Poetry Library, 2023)

The Cost of Avoidance

Steven Hayes, a brilliant clinical psychologist, created Acceptance and Commitment Therapy (ACT). Within this model is the concept of psychological flexibility. Hayes explains it is in the resistance of pain and suffering we cause more pain and suffering (*APA PsycNet.* (n.d.)). Through psychological flexibility, we suffer less and increase our overall happiness and well-being. For example, some of us drink to excess to avoid our negative emotions. When we look at the chemical components of alcohol, it is *poison*. There is no way around this fact, but despite this, drinking is a socially acceptable coping skill. Taking excess amounts of poison over time to avoid feeling discomfort will cause greater suffering, such as cirrhosis of the liver or losing one's job or relationships. Optimal mental health means cognitive flexibility. You will have to learn to accept and feel your emotions despite what society has led you to believe.

If you are experiencing emotional numbness and you suspect this is due to traumatic events or experiences, you will need professional help to unpack your emotions in a safe way. I highly recommend finding a clinician who uses somatic therapy (body sensation) techniques. Why? Because trauma is first experienced (mostly) in the part of the brain responsible for the fight-or-flight response. This means the language of the brainstem and body sensation is speaking with the nervous system. Talking through your emotions and bypassing the physiological response could create a never-ending cycle of re-experiencing the trauma without permanent relief (*Peter Levine on Trauma Healing: A Somatic Approach*, n.d.).

Expressing thoughts, emotions, and feelings is a way we connect as humans. Research indicates these emotionally connected relationships are vital, and a lack of them can be lethal. We all need at least a few friends in our lives with whom we can be authentic, friends who will listen and not give a ton of advice.

White men in the U.S. over the age of sixty-five are currently at the greatest risk of completing suicide. Dr. Sanitato, MD, a geriatric psychiatrist, explains in an interview with The Cleveland Clinic that a major risk factor is the failure to manage after the loss of a spouse. "Let's say someone has been married for forty years, and his wife primarily managed their household. Now that she's died, he's left to his own devices, and he's lost without her. I know that sounds like a stereotype—but it's borne out by the statistics" (Clinic, 2023b).

An article published in 2006 by the Population Reference Bureau (PRB) reviews possible causes contributing to higher levels of suicidality among aging Caucasian men. "Perhaps older men lack the resilience and coping skills of their female counterparts or perhaps it's because men typically have been socialized for power and control. There is certainly a decrease in control within the aging mind and body" (*Elderly White Men Afflicted by High Suicide Rates*, n.d.-b.). I witnessed continuous loss during my time working in the geriatric field. My patients suffered the loss of loved ones, loss of roles within the family, and loss of independence due to illness or aging. Many reported a loss of sense of purpose after retirement.

One of my primary goals for treatment when working with seniors was to increase socialization and connection. PRB goes on to explain that Latin cultures place a higher level of value on close family relationships, which may explain why suicide rates are substantially lower among this population (Clinic, 2023b). As we have discussed previously, we need people; we need real connections. This means empathy, respect, physical touch, feeling seen and heard, and providing this connection for our loved ones in return. If you are feeling empty, chances are, you need more connection in your life. I recognize this means more vulnerability and more discomfort. This takes real strength and courage. I'll leave you with another of my favorite quotes from Col. Grossman: "No macho men and no pity parties" (Grossman & Christensen, 2008). Don't allow the Man Box to shut out your humanity, and don't let your emotions cripple you. If they do, just make sure to get back up. It's okay to ask for help.

In the next chapter, we will discuss what's inside the Pink Box, a.k.a. female gender role expectations. You may be tempted to skip ahead, but don't. The next chapter will give you a better understanding of your partner and equip you with more patience, as well as compassion, for the women in your life. This is a vital part of working toward a healthy relationship.

NOTES :

CHAPTER 3:

The "F" Word (by Stephanie)

"If we empower women to work outside the house without expecting men to work inside the house, then we aren't empowering women. We're exploiting them."
– Forida D.

It's a hot summer's day in the early 1980s in Taylorsville, Utah, and I am about five years old. I'm outside with Tony, a neighbor boy who is the same age as me. His house is just five houses down from mine, so we can often be found together. We've been playing yard games like tag and leapfrog for the past hour. We are both sweating and out of breath from all the active play as well as from being in the hot sun. Tony is a round, short boy with dark hair and caramel-colored skin. He stands with his bare feet in the green, freshly cut grass in his front yard. He wears a dinosaur T-shirt and loose athletic shorts. In contrast, I am a very blond and pale stick-like girl with unevenly cut bangs that are too long and get in my eyes when I run. I am wearing a My Little Pony T-shirt and bright pink shorts. I am also barefoot and had kicked my shoes off when the games began.

Tony is panting hard and takes off his T-shirt, wiping his sweaty forehead with it. I think to myself that this is a *really* good idea, so I do the same. I'm standing there in the grass smiling with Tony for less than a minute before his father comes running out of their house, yelling, "Put your shirt back on!" looking directly at me. Confused, Tony and I looked at him, his angry face turning red, and then at each other. I can feel the heat of embarrassment rising in my cheeks, and Tony's face looks like I had better listen to his father "or else." I hurriedly picked my shirt up off the ground and put it back on, not wanting to get in trouble. Tony's father says something in Spanish that I don't understand and then sternly in English, "Girls *do not* take their shirts off!" before he turns on his heel and goes back into the house with the screen door slamming.

This is one of my earliest memories of realizing that I was being treated differently for no other reason other than because I was female. I've had countless more experiences in the 40-plus years I have lived my life, but this one stands out. Perhaps it was because I really had no idea at the time what the problem was, and in many ways, I still don't. After all, Tony and I looked essentially the same as children without our shirts on. I certainly did not have anything that resembled breasts, no more than Tony did, anyway. His father's response was one of anger and disgust, and I remember running home to my mother in tears.

I bet if you ask any woman you know, they could give many examples of similar gender othering experiences. These examples would describe how females within our culture are separated from men as a way to place them within a lower status. My story is a relatively tame one, but you might hear some that are far more disturbing should you get the courage or curiosity to ask. What is this phenomenon, you may be wondering? It is what is known as *patriarchy*. According to Science Direct, "Patriarchy is a system of relationships, beliefs, and values embedded in political, social, and economic systems that structure gender inequality between men and women. Attributes seen as 'feminine' or pertaining to women are undervalued, while attributes regarded as 'masculine' or pertaining to men are privileged" (Nash, 2009). So, when did patriarchy become such an integrated part of our world? Well, I'll give you an extremely condensed version of the history of the patriarchy for the purpose of this book.

According to Angela Saini, author of *The Patriarchs, The Origins of Inequality*, we were not always a patriarchy. In fact, "women in matrilineal societies, such as Nairs of Kerala, the Khasis of Meghalaya, or the Mosuo of Western China, have often exercised (and in some cases still do) considerable freedom around sex, labor, child rearing and property" (Saini, 2023).

In 1884, Frederich Engels published a theory that stated that matriarchs were primitive and that to be more civilized, societies would need to become composed of "patriarchal monogamous families" (Saini, 2023). Saini also reports that there was not one single event that defeated these matriarchies, but there were many over centuries that were related to "societal pressures that filtered down into households, affecting power dynamics inside relationships" (Saini, 2023). After this theory and others like it were published, the laws in Europe and eventually the United States regarding land ownership, inheritance, and marriage began to change giving men more power over women. This was justified as being more progressive because men were seen as being more rational than their female counterparts.

In response to patriarchy, eventually came the birth of the feminist movement, or "feminism." Feminism can be traced all the way back to ancient Greece when Plato himself advocated for women to have equal rights in governing and even defending Greece. In the 1800s, famous suffragette women such as Elizabeth Cady Stanton and Lucretia Mott began to fight for women's rights to vote in America.

However, the vote wasn't granted until 1920, after women's participation in World War I had shown they had *earned* the right to vote.

During the Great Depression, many men lost their jobs, and women joined the workforce doing domestic or secretarial jobs, which were considered "women's work" and generally paid lower wages but were more stable at the time. During World War II, women actively worked in the military or took over factory jobs previously reserved for men. When the war ended, they were forced out of these jobs and expected to return to the household or to take on "women's work" again. Many women wanted to remain in the factories' higher-paying jobs. Those allowed to stay were typically offered lower wages than their male counterparts.

After the Civil Rights Movement in 1954 came the Equal Pay Act of 1963, which was an attempt to ensure that men and women received equal pay for the same work done by their male counterparts. In 1972, the Equal Rights Amendment was passed to ensure equality between the sexes, but it was not ratified by enough states to become law. One year later, Roe V. Wade was passed to ensure a woman's right to choose abortion.

In 2010, the #MeToo movement spotlighted current "rape culture" and sexual assault against women as well as the work still needed to combat misogyny in America and around the world. On January 21, 2017, hundreds of thousands of people participated in The Women's March in Washington, D.C., to protest perceived threats to reproductive, human, and civil rights by a new governing administration that had just taken office. These fears were realized when Roe V. Wade was overturned on June 24, 2022. Not only do women have fewer reproductive rights today, but women also still earn less pay than their male counterparts. According to an article from the Pew Research Center, "In 2022, women typically earned 82 cents for every dollar earned by men" (Greenwood, 2023a). In my home state of Utah, we currently have one of the largest gender pay gaps in the nation. Women earn an average of 30% less than men (Madsen, 2021). This is common for states with large religious populations (Jacobs, 2021).

You may be asking yourself why we are including the history of patriarchy and feminism in this book and, more importantly, why it should matter to you. The long answer to that question is that to achieve equality among the genders, we must understand how patriarchy began as a social construct and how it is reinforced today. Only then can we hope to dismantle it. The short answer is simply this: *Patriarchy hurts men, too*. That's right, it's not a good thing for anyone, man or woman.

A 2019 article in the Washington Post titled "Why the Patriarchy is Killing Men" explains that in patriarchal or more "traditional" societies, men have shorter life spans than their female counterparts. They are more likely to die by suicide, avoid seeking help for both medical and mental health problems, have access to firearms, and are more likely to engage in dangerous risk-taking behaviors. This same article also reports that men who earned less than their spouses for an extended period of time showed "shorter life expectancy and increased chances of cardiovascular problems like diabetes, heart disease, high cholesterol, hypertension and stroke" due to the "loss of connection to their identity as breadwinners" (Plank, 2019). Recent research done by Daniel Coleman of Fordham University on 2,431 young adults 18 to 19 years old "found that men who identified with rigid beliefs — that men must provide at any cost, be invulnerable or be self-sufficient — were more likely to have suicidal thoughts and exhibit signs of depression" (Coleman, 2015).

Now, let's float back to the scenario in Chapter 1 with our business partners. Do you remember that your friend was doing all the physical labor and taking on the majority of the mental and emotional load as well? You had admitted that you felt these tasks were "beneath you" and that it was "his job, anyway." Now, I want you to have a moment of *complete honesty* with yourself. Don't worry, this is just between you and *you*. Ask yourself now if you have ever used the same or similar justifications for why you do not take on certain household chores or some of the mental or emotional load at home. Have you ever thought, "That's *her* job," or "Men don't do that kind of thing," or something similar? If the answer is yes, then there is a clear hierarchy between men and women within your own belief system, and the work to challenge that can now begin. Hooray!! Don't worry, you won't have to do this alone. We will give you a handy dandy guide to help you get on the right path in future chapters. Hang in there!

NOTES :

CHAPTER 4:

What Does "Emotionally Unavailable" Mean? (by Stacy)

"Emotions can help you and they can hurt you but you have no say in the matter until you understand them."
– Travis Bradberry

In April of 2023, an article appeared in Psychology Today Magazine titled "Men: Understanding Male Emotions." This particular article not only got my attention but sparked the idea for this book.

Within this article, male clinicians share insights into why men often struggle with emotional expression. Assael Romanelli, PhD, highlights that boys are socialized to prioritize toughness, teamwork, stoicism, and competition, which discourages emotional vulnerability. Despite being born as emotionally sensitive as girls, societal expectations lead men to repress feelings, causing a disconnect from themselves and others. Romanelli describes how this can lead to a form of covert depression, where men experience the world as dull and unfulfilling, a perception their partners may misinterpret as stoicism or disinterest (Assael, 2023).

Avrum Weiss, PhD, adds that men often lack confidence in handling relationship conflicts, fearing that expressing needs might worsen situations. He notes that men are socialized to feel responsible for their partner's happiness, and a partner's dissatisfaction can feel like personal failure. This fear can lead men to avoid discussions altogether, feeling too intimidated to address relationship issues. Weiss shares that men frequently feel apprehensive about voicing concerns with their partners, fearing the potential negative impact (Weiss, 2023).

When I read this statement from Weiss, I thought with disbelief, "*Men* are afraid of *women*?!" I want to be clear here that I'm not speaking about men who are in relationships with narcissistic or abusive women because, let's be honest, those women *are* scary. What I found particularly surprising about Weiss's statement is that, as discussed in Chapter 4 of this book, men hold the majority of power in our culture. Statistically speaking, men abuse and kill women at higher rates, they hold the majority of wealth in our country, and they occupy the majority of leadership roles at both state and national levels. In 2022, five men and only one woman changed women's reproductive rights in our country (Coates, 2023). Five men who don't have a vagina or uterus decided the rights of these reproductive organs. Again, how is it that men are afraid to approach the women in their lives about the problems within their relationships when they hold so much power?

Why, in particular, do men feel they are perpetually at risk for being in "the doghouse," and how does that relate to the mental load and emotional labor? I myself suspect this unease is that men have an underlying awareness of the inequality within their relationships. They may be unaware of the depth of the emotional labor and mental load their partner carries, but they can see the signs of burnout happening in their partners. So, without full awareness, they may believe their partner's dissatisfaction is due to poor communication, perfectionism, or some other kind of pathology. I wonder how many marriages have failed unnecessarily due to the lack of awareness that women are culturally set up for burnout and that men are living on the surface level of life.

You may have sensed at times that your partner is approaching "the end of their rope" with frustrations within the relationship but did not exactly know how to help her. Maybe you have attempted to help by picking a task you felt confident you could do but felt hurt when you didn't receive praise or recognition when it was completed. Maybe you have asked your partner for instructions or where items were kept in the home in order to complete the task, only to be met with anger or frustration from her. Maybe you completed a task, but your partner told you it was done incorrectly and was angry because now she has to "do it all over again." All of these scenarios are common but very problematic. We will address how to better address these particular issues later, so hold tight.

Perhaps another component of this fear described by Weiss is that men also don't know what to do when emotions are elevated. If men cannot tolerate vulnerable emotions and, therefore, avoid any discussion or conflict, that is a problem. How will couples compromise, repair, and build a fulfilling relationship if one partner is afraid of the other? Or worse, both are afraid? I think this fear and avoidance is actually more common than we realize.

Learning to manage the negative feelings and emotions that come up in a relationship is imperative to the health and success of that relationship. This is a basic skill we all need as humans! In his book *ACT With Love,* author Russ Harris explains that "avoiding conflict is living in the comfort zone." He also states, "Unfortunately the comfort zone is not that comfortable. The more you live in it, the more you feel stuck, weighed down, defeated by life… If you always avoid these situations your relationship is doomed to stagnation" (R. Harris, 2009). Terry Real, a prominent couples counselor and expert in men's psychology, states that "in a real marriage, heat comes from heat. Real passion comes right out of real conflict, full engagement, taking each other on… Smooth functioning avoidance is romantic death. Partners need to rough it up now and then to go deeper" (Real, T. 2022). One of my clients recently told me she read somewhere that 8 out of 11 interactions in a relationship should be positive. I think I'd agree with this. Once we get to a healthy place in our relationship, most interactions should be positive or neutral. You can't avoid the three negative interactions. That's just life. You are two different people with different personalities and life experiences. Conflict and disagreements will happen. That said, these negative interactions should not involve abuse. Most couples counselors will refer out to clinicians or programs who focus on and specialize in domestic violence (DV) if abuse is happening within the relationship. We will discuss components of abuse in Chapter 7 so you can find appropriate support if this is of concern to you.

A common myth within the general population is that abuse stems from anger management issues. Anger management can be part of why the abuse is happening, but it is not the core cause. Before we move on to discussing all emotions, let's discuss anger. I feel this is probably the most common emotion men are easily able to identify and feel, but they may not always know what to do with it. Some men are afraid of anger if they have experienced others using it to fuel violence. They may have worked hard to stuff it down. To compartmentalize it and never deal with it. As we discussed earlier, there is a cost to this approach. Eventually, you begin to feel numb with all emotions, good or bad. Your body pays the price as well. It's like your sewer backing up. Those emotions have to go somewhere, and they will inevitably show up in your body through pain or disease.

Some men may deal with a disagreement by embracing the emotion of anger. This is because anger is a socially accepted emotion for men to display. It can also be intoxicating to a degree. It feels good to vent your frustrations by yelling loudly, slamming a cupboard door, or throwing something and watching it shatter. However, if you behave in these ways, you will most likely experience shame afterward. Eww, shame! You will also have a more emotionally distant partner because they will view you as unsafe or volatile. The cost of these behaviors to your relationship is simply too high.

Anger is perfectly okay to feel, but it's not okay to harm or control others with it. Anger will often show up when we feel like we are losing control or a goal is blocked. Unfortunately, we have little control over anything in this life, so anger isn't achieving this goal anyhow. If your partner or child falls in line when you get angry, you may feel like you are in control, but this is a mirage. What you are doing is causing distance and compliance through fear. If you find yourself identifying with this, keep reading because we will discuss this in detail in the parenting chapter. So remember, the only thing you have a modicum of control over in this life is yourself. This is why I believe you can work *with* anger instead of embracing it or bottling it up. Terrence Real explains this pivot in automatic behavior to intentional team effort as *relational heroism and relational mindfulness*: "That moment when every muscle and nerve in your body is screaming to do the sample old, but through raised consciousness, insight, discipline and grace, you lift yourself off your accustomed track and deliberately place yourself on another track... stopping for a brief moment and centering ourselves... observing thoughts, feeling and impulses and choosing something different" (Real, T. 2022). This, of course, takes time and practice, but behaviors and automatic reactions can change over time.

It's best to practice any new skills in the beginning while *not* upset. This will increase the likelihood that you will remember these skills when you are in distress. If you wait until you are angry to use them, you will probably revert to old habits. Here are a few tools to get started. You may want to expand on these in therapy.

Anger Management Tools & Skills:

Make a List

Write a list of things that tend to make you angry, annoyed, or irritated. These are often described as triggers. Here are a few examples:

- People cutting me off in traffic.
- People talking over me.
- My partner leaving hair in the shower drain.

Write a Script:

Once you have a list of triggers, imagine scenarios in which they occur. Then, mentally write a script for how you would like to respond and behave when triggered. This means behaving in an *appropriate* way, i.e., feeling angry but not doing harm with it. Visualize being able to say, "I respectfully disagree," then calmly walking away from your obnoxious coworker. Imagine pausing, taking a breath, and telling your partner, "I need a time-out to think about this. Let's talk about this after dinner." These imagined scenarios don't need to be too complicated or detailed. Just keep it simple. If you are wondering why this actually helps, let's review a study involving weight training and visualization.

A study in 2020 conducted by Transylvania University recruited 133 students in the Transylvania University strength training program. Participants were told to visualize themselves lifting 110% of their max weight for at least five minutes a day. They were instructed to imagine lifting the weight with proper form, speed, and confidence. After just three weeks, the test group increased their max weight by an average of ten pounds. The control group increased their weight by five pounds. This indicates that simply by visualizing lifting more weight, the test group was able to increase their weight by an average of twice the amount of the control group (Hynes et al., 2020). Perhaps you think visualizations are just hippy-dippy BS, but trust me, it works! Why? Because most brains are great at visualizing scenarios in great detail. This is why so many of us are terrified of heights. When standing next to a cliff, we can literally imagine in detail what it would feel like to fall to our deaths. This is so you can prepare if you should fall. So, why not use the brain's power of visualizing scenarios for good versus worry? Below is an explanation of how to create a visualization. Feel free to write your scripts in a notebook for safekeeping and to help you remember.

Traffic: *Someone just cut you off.*

Imagine you are able to take a few deep breaths, then tune back into the radio program you were enjoying. Imagine how your body will feel moving from anger to relaxation. Notice your muscles relaxing and your heartbeat slowing. Notice the temperature inside the car and the colors outside your windshield; imagine the speaker's soothing voice coming through the radio. Practice these visualizations for at least a few minutes a day.

Create a Mantra:

This is a word or phrase you can repeat to remind yourself why managing your anger in a healthy way is important to you. Here are a few you might use:

- I will protect my peace by letting go of anger.
- This feeling will pass.
- I want my partner to feel safe.
- It's not about me.
- I am calm and in control.
- I breathe in anger and exhale calm.
- Notice how little they are (your children).

Breathe:

Inhale, and as you do, inflate the belly. Place your hand on your stomach to feel it rise. As you exhale, imagine you are breathing through a straw. You will pucker your lips into a small O as you exhale. It is important to slow the exhalation as this will help send the message to your brain that you are safe. Complete as many rounds of this breath until you feel grounded.

Reframe:

If anger tends to arise because of thoughts such as, "He thinks I'm an idiot," "She doesn't respect me," or "He's so (insert criticism here)," whatever the negative thoughts about others are, you may need to practice these two skills.

1. **Give People the Benefit of the Doubt**. That's it. Simply begin practicing viewing the people in your life through an accepting lens. This doesn't mean you accept and ignore toxic behavior. This means generally believing our loved ones and *most* people are good, kind, and human. They make mistakes. They aren't out to get you. So practice thinking things like, "She must have been busy and forgot," or "Maybe that guy is driving like a jerk because he's on his way to the hospital to say goodbye to a loved one."

2. **Don't Take Things Personally**. I know this is easier said than done. My favorite resource for remembering this concept is within the text of *The Four Agreements.*

The Four Agreements is a wonderful book by Don Miguel Ruiz. In this book, he discusses four truths, one of which is not taking things personally. Archaeologists discovered these four agreements when researching the ancient Toltec people of Mexico. Plaques throughout the excavated village explained these agreements as a guide for living a happy life. Ruiz discusses them in detail in his book, but I have provided a summary of them below for our purposes.

1. ***Be impeccable with your word:*** *Speak plainly and with integrity; don't gossip or speak unkindly of yourself or others.*
2. ***Don't take anything personally*****:** *Being a victim of others' judgment is suffering. What others think and say is a reflection of their reality. Even if what they say is kind, it's about them, not you. "I may compliment you because it makes me feel good to see you smile. I may insult you because…"*
3. ***Don't make assumptions:*** *Ask questions, be brave, and speak clearly to avoid miscommunication.*
4. ***Always do your best:*** *Do your best and accept your best might change if you're ill, etc. If you do your best, you will avoid self-judgment.*

(Miguel Ruiz, D. 1997)

These four agreements are wonderful for letting go of self-judgment and judgment of others. You may write these down on a piece of paper and stick them on your refrigerator to help you remember them.

Check In with Your Inner Toddler:

Sometimes anger is more about unmet needs. When we have a toddler melting down, we know it's time to ask if they are tired, hungry, thirsty, lonely, bored, overwhelmed (too much noise, too many people around, etc.), or need the bathroom. Guess what? In this way, we are all toddlers. If you are feeling irritable, ask yourself these same questions. Then, meet your needs so you can think and behave like an adult again. Hey, have a cookie and a nap if you need it. No judgment here.

Lemon Squeezes:

Imagine you have a lemon in each hand. Ball up your fist tightly and count slowly to 30. Then release them. Repeat until you feel better.

Move Your Body:

I highly recommend this approach if you tend to behave in scary ways when angry: if you yell, call names, or throw things. Sometimes it's best to just remove ourselves from a situation. I also suggest you warn your partner that you are going to start physically removing yourself to calm down, but you will return when you are stable. It can be scary for a partner who doesn't know what is happening to see their partner literally run away. They might be afraid you won't come back.

Do jumping jacks, wall push-ups, or run around the block. Anger creates energy, and we need to release it, so find what works for you! Bonus, you may end up healthier, and the endorphins from exercise can feel pretty good.

I feel it is important to mention that many men of color do not feel safe expressing anger, as this can literally cost them their lives. They are taught by loving parents or caregivers to not show or express anger. This is due to stereotypes and stigma embedded in our dominant culture that men of color are dangerous, criminals, or gang members, etc.

So, in a nutshell, we have a huge population of people who are emotionally constipated or only express negative emotions in destructive ways. We must create a culture where we are allowed to feel all our emotions and learn to express them in more appropriate ways. Let's move on to our other basic emotions and how to begin living the full human experience.

Emotional Intelligence (EQ) & Emotion Regulation:

Dr. John Gottman states, "The more emotionally intelligent a couple, the better able they are to understand, honor, and respect each other and their marriage" (Gottman, J. & Silver, N., 2015). So, why are emotions important? Remember, emotions are just messengers. They give us information. We don't need to let them cripple us. We need to feel them, listen to them, and move forward. When we avoid feeling our emotions, we can get stuck in them. Sadness can turn into depression, fear can turn into panic, and anger can turn into rage. In the book *Emotional Intelligence 2.0*, Travis Bradberry defines emotional intelligence

(EQ) as having four components: personal competence, social competence, self-awareness, and self-management skills. Personal competence involves being aware of your emotions and the ability to manage them effectively. Social competence involves understanding others' emotions, behaviors, and moods in order to enhance the quality of your relationship (Bradberry T. & Greaves, J., 2009). You may want to pick up a copy of *Emotional Intelligence 2.0* for an in-depth explanation and working model to increase your EQ. Below are our favorite tools for increasing emotional intelligence and regulation.

First Notice:

Take some time throughout the day to notice what emotions you feel. You could put a reminder on your phone every hour or a sticky note somewhere you will see throughout the day. Stick to basic emotions for now. Observe happiness, fear, anger, envy, disgust, sadness, and shame… and notice where they show up in your body. Notice how long each emotion lasts or if you are experiencing a few at the same time. I know this noticing sounds strange, but this is part of emotional intelligence. Emotions show up as physical body responses. Begin to notice how your body feels when an emotion arises. This will help you better regulate them before they take over. I will list where each emotion may show up to help you better identify them.

Emotions and Their Physical Symptoms:

1. **Anger:** Manifested by tight muscles, a clenching jaw, a flushed face, and a racing heart. Emotions may feel explosive, with a desire to cry or act out physically.
2. **Disgust:** Characterized by nausea, gagging, and avoidance behaviors. It may prompt a need to escape, feel contaminated, or destroy something unpleasant.
3. **Envy:** Involves muscle tension, stomach discomfort, and clenching teeth. It may lead to a desire for others to lose what they have or motivation to improve themselves.
4. **Fear:** Exhibits as shortness of breath, rapid heartbeat, tight muscles, and a need to scream or run. Cold sweats, nausea, and a choking sensation are also common.
5. **Happiness:** Associated with excitement, energy, laughter, flushed cheeks, and playfulness. It often leads to connection and feeling open, with gestures like hugging and sharing.
6. **Jealousy:** Shows through tight muscles, rapid breathing, and clenching teeth. Emotional symptoms include suspicion, pride, helplessness, and a need for control.
7. **Love:** Marked by energy, eye contact, touching, smiling, and a desire to spend time with the loved one, often including physical affection.

8. **Sadness:** Leads to lethargy, a sense of emptiness, chest heaviness, tearfulness, and dizziness.
9. **Shame:** Felt as a pit in the stomach, dread, and a desire to hide or disappear.
10. **Guilt:** Causes a flushed face, nervousness, and a feeling of suffocation.

Summary:

- Emotional intelligence is just as important as intellectual intelligence.
- Avoiding negative emotions and interactions will lead to stagnation in your relationship.
- Work with anger, not against it.
- Use your body to release negative emotions from your body. This can be done through physical movement and breathwork.
- Visualizations can help the nervous system release emotions.
- Trapped emotions wreak havoc on the body.
- Anger creates energy. Don't use this energy as a weapon.

NOTES :

CHAPTER 5:

When You Think You're Okay, But You're Not Okay (by Stacy)

The Trauma Connection

Stephanie and I are both trauma-informed mental health clinicians. This means we focus on helping clients heal from difficult experiences in their lives so they can live a happier, healthier existence. We believe trauma is at the heart of many mental, emotional, and physical pains we experience as human beings. None of us get to adulthood without *some* trauma. Okay, before you flip out, give us some time to explain: Trauma may not be what you think it is. The Greek word for wound is trauma ("Trauma," 2024). We can think of trauma as physical or emotional wounds sustained from stressors throughout our lifetime. *Stressors* are stimuli our brains deem as threatening to some degree. These include certain sights, sounds, smells, textures, etc. This is why we believe it is vital to use tools geared toward managing the aftereffects of these common daily experiences. In the next chapter, we will provide you with basic tools compiled over our combined 20+ years of clinical work to help deal with some of life's biggest challenges. But before we move on to the toolbox, let's first discuss the brain and body connection so you can fully understand why this work is so important.

If you want to show up for your partner as the best version of you, it's going to require taking good care of yourself. If you are in pain, fatigued, or stressed, you will not be able to navigate disagreements well. You will be mentally, physically, and emotionally unavailable to meet your partner's needs or verbalize your own in a kind and respectful manner. That said, deeper "trauma work" will need to be done with a skilled and knowledgeable mental health clinician. Until then, this chapter should give you a good understanding of the value behind healing past wounds. So, let's get back to the big question: What exactly is trauma?

We often think trauma has to be an intense experience with extreme violence resulting in death or physical harm, such as combat or car accidents. Unfortunately, trauma happens more often than you might think. I define trauma as any time your sympathetic nervous system (SNS) was activated too often, at too high an intensity, or for too long. Your SNS is the part of our nervous system responsible for triggering our survival responses. It's part of our internal alarm system, and its job is to trigger our fight-or-flight reflexes (Britannica, 2024, Jan 8). This means that if, as a child, you had a parent who yelled at you, often ignored you, or spanked you, or if you were bullied, didn't fit in with your peers, struggled with math, etc., you could have unresolved trauma. This is because the SNS can overwhelm your brain's ability to make sense of these experiences.

Resilience, or the ability to cope, often depends on having enough support after a stressor is introduced. When we don't get that needed support, the parts of our brain responsible for processing information can get stuck. This is why researchers think flashbacks occur. It's the brain repeating sensory information over and over in an attempt to make sense of it. If this overwhelm happens enough, this can cause permanent changes in the brain's structure. We call this the "amygdala hijack."

Our amygdala is a part of the brain located in the middle front area. It's a paired structure, meaning you have one located on the left and right sides of the inner brain. Its primary function is to receive sensory information in order to modulate decision-making, memory, and attention (Salzman, 2016). The amygdala is part of the limbic system, which is responsible for emotions, motivation, sense of smell, behavior, and memory. Structures within the limbic system include interconnected parts: the thalamus, hypothalamus, basal ganglia, cingulate gyrus, hippocampus, and, as stated, the amygdala (Raikar, 2024).

A study conducted in 2012 looked at 99 combat veterans with a Post-Traumatic Stress Disorder (PTSD) diagnosis. The finding of the study showed a larger volume of the amygdala than participants without a PTSD diagnosis. This may indicate the amygdala increases in volume due to hypersensitivity if one is exposed repeatedly to traumatic events throughout their lifetime (Kuo et al., 2012). This can lead to what is known as conditioning. This means the brain has been conditioned to respond in a certain way to the same or similar stimuli. It is like the brain's alarm system literally gets bigger, louder, and more reactive each time it's activated. This may explain the symptoms of PTSD, including hypervigilance, believing the world is a bad place, as well as feelings of impending doom. This is like when you burn the toast, and the smoke alarm goes off. It's a bit of an overreaction by the smoke detector. You might not like the smell of burnt toast, but you don't need to get everyone out of the house for leaving the bread in the toaster too long.

The brain collects data throughout your life to determine what is safe and what is dangerous. The SNS is activated within milliseconds to manage these potential threats. When the SNS is triggered, the hormones adrenaline and cortisol are released. If enough cortisol and adrenaline are released enough or too often, they act as acid running through the body. It can literally break down the body at a cellular level.

Emily Nagoski states in her book *Burnout,* "Chronically activated stress response means chronically increased blood pressure, which is like constantly turning a firehose on your blood vessels…increased wear and tear on your blood vessels leads to chronic illness." She further explains that human beings get stuck in the stress response, which negatively impacts digestion, immune functioning, hormones, and every organ in the body. This is how chronic stress leads to threatening illness (Nagoski, E. & Nagoski, A., 2019).

These hormones are important if you come across a grizzly bear on the hiking trail or for dodging bullets in battle. They allow you to fight or flee by relaying messages throughout the body to help you react quickly. However, adrenaline and cortisol are not so helpful if they continue to be pumped through your body day in and day out at high levels. Unfortunately for humans, our nervous system doesn't know the difference between a grizzly looking for lunch or an angry text from your partner. This is why many of us live with chronic stress and may not even be aware of it. Our amygdala may respond to a gigantic list of sights, sounds, smells, textures, etc., it has deemed as dangerous due to past experiences. Over time, we can get stuck in permanent hypervigilance, which is the feeling that something bad is about to happen, so you can never fully relax. The problem is that we need our sympathetic nervous system to respond to danger but not to believe everything and everyone is a potential threat. That's exhausting!

More bad news: Our nervous systems are terrible at getting back to baseline if this system is activated too much. This means serious long-term effects on our physical and mental well-being. The Mayo Clinic explains chronic stress can be a key factor in the onset of health problems, including digestive issues, chronic headaches, muscle tension pain, heart disease, heart attacks, sleep issues, weight gain, and difficulties with memory and focus (*Chronic Stress Puts Your Health at Risk*, 2023). This is because, as we discussed previously, chronic stress activates the SNS, which releases hormones that break down the body over time. I rarely have a client on my caseload who doesn't have some form of chronic pain or illness. I believe this is due to exposure to stressors throughout their lifetime without enough support to create resiliency. Stress gets stuck in the body, and the alarm system gets hypersensitive, resulting in more wear and tear.

Okay, now here is the good news: Through the magic of science and research, we now know the brain has the amazing ability to heal and repair itself through *neuroplasticity*. PubMed defines neuroplasticity as "the ability of the nervous system to change its activity in response to intrinsic or extrinsic stimuli by reorganizing its structure, organization or connections" (*Neuroplasticity*, 2024). This means working to regulate or soothe our nervous system routinely can change how stimuli are processed in the mind and body. Basically, you can hold on to stress, or you can help yourself release it. Turn to the next chapter to learn all the ways you can reduce the sensitivity of your amygdala and reduce those nasty hormones that are wreaking havoc on your body and brain.

NOTES :

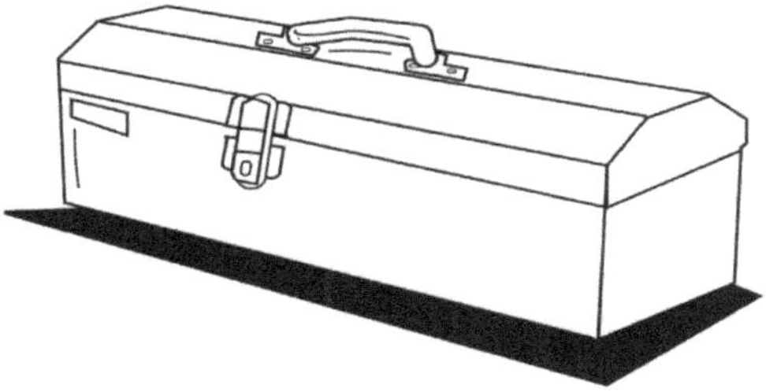

CHAPTER 6:
Your New Toolbox (by Stacy & Stephanie)

Today, trauma-informed therapists know the best interventions for treating trauma are geared toward helping you feel safe in your body again. You may be thinking, "What are you talking about? I am perfectly safe in my body?" Don't forget that your nervous system has memory. If your brain has activated the stress response cycle enough times, your body will feel unsafe, unstable, and unpredictable. This stress response becomes easier to trigger the more times it's activated, just like the toaster and the smoke alarm we discussed in the previous chapter.

This chapter is a "toolbox" of exercises and techniques to calm the nervous system that, over time, can give you more control over your mind and body. We have also included important components for positive change in your life and relationship. You can play with these techniques over the coming weeks. Perhaps you choose one a week to practice daily. This will allow you to compile a list of your favorite coping skills, and you won't have to think so hard about what to do when in distress. Set aside the rest. Everyone is different, so take time to figure out what works best for you.

We have broken up this chapter into three parts: Nervous System Support & Reset, Effective Communication, and How to Fight Fair. Although we have included a quick and dirty explanation of our favorite tools and resources, there are many more. A mental health clinician will also help you expand your toolbox.

Nervous System Support & Reset

Somatic Exercises & the Vagus Nerve:

The Vagus nerve is the longes t nerve system in your body. It has many functions, but perhaps one of the most important is that it stimulates the Parasympathetic Nervous System (PNS). When the PNS is stimulated, it activates your body's own calming response. This works by slowing your heart rate, increasing digestion, and dropping your blood pressure. Somatic exercise can stimulate the Vagus nerve and, therefore, the PNS.

Disclaimer: Before engaging in any new exercise program, make sure to speak with your primary care physician to receive physical clearance. This will help avoid injury or other health complications.

Somatic Therapy vs. Yoga:

As a trained yoga instructor, Stacy often combines yoga and somatic therapies when working with her clients. We believe it is important to offer regular yoga practice as an option for clients because it can be a wonderful way of fostering a healthier lifestyle and healing the nervous system. Research shows yoga can help slow aging, increase brain functioning, and lower the intensity and severity of several health conditions (*Yoga for Health: What the Science Says*, n.d.).

Somatic exercises involve the use of the mind–body connection to release stress or emotional pain trapped in the body. Somatic movement is similar to yoga, but somatic therapy utilizes slower micro-movements with an individualized approach (Clara, 2023). Yoga typically involves mindfulness and periods of movement, stretching, sitting in stillness, and holding specific poses while simultaneously pairing movement with breath. In yoga, breathing is viewed as our greatest source of energy. Breathing techniques are often incorporated into yoga practice. Yoga also has a spiritual component, encouraging students to foster personal spirituality regardless of religious affiliation. Yoga is an ancient practice; some historians believe it existed before Jesus walked Earth. Somatic therapy has roots in yoga but is somewhat newer to the therapy world.

Today, trauma-informed yoga classes are taught all over the country. Some yoga programs are specific to certain populations, such as sexual assault victims, veterans, or traumatic brain injury (TBI) survivors. There is face yoga, chair yoga, laughing yoga, goat yoga, etc. If you enjoy some of the somatic poses below, you may want to consider adding a beginner's yoga class to your toolbox. Trained body-focused therapists utilize and teach somatic in session.

The somatic poses below are, in fact, also yoga poses, and we have chosen poses most likely to help with a variety of emotional and psychological pain. Somatic exercises calm and heal the body by repairing the damage done by stress or traumatic experiences through energy release. Below is an example of how effective somatic work can be.

Jessica: (Stacy's Client)

I began seeing Jessica after all medical causes for her chronic leg pain had been ruled out by her medical team, and she was advised to seek the help of a mental health professional. After years of treatment, they suspected her pain was related to unresolved childhood trauma.

When we first met, Jessica was in her late twenties, single, and new to her career in finance. She had been attending physical therapy regularly for over two years. Unsurprisingly, she had tried several other medical treatments with little success and had now exhausted her options.

Jessica had two younger brothers, and their parents divorced when Jessica was in high school. Jessica's parents had agreed to share custody after the divorce, and from the information I gathered in our sessions, Jessica's father appeared to have narcissistic tendencies.

Jessica's father would often praise her for her beauty (usually around family and friends). He would, however, quickly point out how "trashy" she looked if wearing clothing that showed any of her body's feminine features. Humiliating her in public was a common occurrence when she was with him. Jessica's father was extremely strict when it came to her grades, and he would belittle her for hours if she received anything less than the highest grades.

Both of her parents expected Jessica to be responsible for her younger brothers. This allowed her very little time to study or to have a normal social life. If she hadn't been involved in theater and debate, she would have been a very lonely teen. Despite the hefty responsibility on her shoulders, Jessica was a straight-A student.

Her mother struggled with depression her entire life, and Jessica had many memories of her mother refusing to get out of bed. Jessica told me during one session that her mother "would go to work, come home, and retreat to her room, so it was on me to feed my brothers dinner and help them with homework." The divorce between her parents happened after her father had cheated on her mother multiple times. After being confronted by her mother about his cheating, her father had an angry, explosive reaction and stormed out of the house. He moved out of the family home shortly after that and resumed his life with no regret or compassion for the hurt he had inflicted on Jessica's mother.

After the divorce, Jessica's parents used her as their personal therapist. They told her horrifying details about their relationship and expected her to pick sides. Her father would lecture her for hours on how awful her mother was, and she spent many nights holding her mother while she sobbed uncontrollably.

Jessica had grown up in an environment where she was trapped. Through somatic work, I helped her escape. I told her to visualize the most intense memories of wanting to run away from her father's rantings or her mother's dependency. Then, using micro-movements, she would run in slow motion around the coffee table in my small office while visualizing running away from her parents. I had her practice this when she went jogging, as I knew she enjoyed running for exercise. It was not long before she began to experience a significant decrease in the discomfort in her legs. These exercises allowed her brain to complete the stress cycle and release the emotional pain tied to the traumatic memories. This story is just one example of how powerful somatic movement can be for healing trauma. Now, let's explore other somatic methods that can help regulate the nervous system and promote healing.

Deep Breathing:

There are specific types of breathing exercises that stimulate the body's calming response. There are many scripts for breathing out there, but perhaps the simplest is known as triangle breathing (see the illustration below). The three most important things to remember with any deep breathing exercise are: 1) Breathe in through your nose and out through your mouth; 2) each breath out should be longer than the breath in; 3) your stomach should be rising and falling with each breath in and out. This shows you are breathing with your diaphragm and not from your chest, which can cause hyperventilation.

If you want to practice this technique, lie flat on your back with a small item on your stomach, such as a pillow or plastic cup, and watch it go up and down in tandem with your breath. Breathe in for a count of four, then hold your breath for a count of four, and last, breathe out for a count of five. Repeat. We recommend you practice 20 minutes per day, about five minutes at a time. Do not wait until you are anxious to practice your breathing.

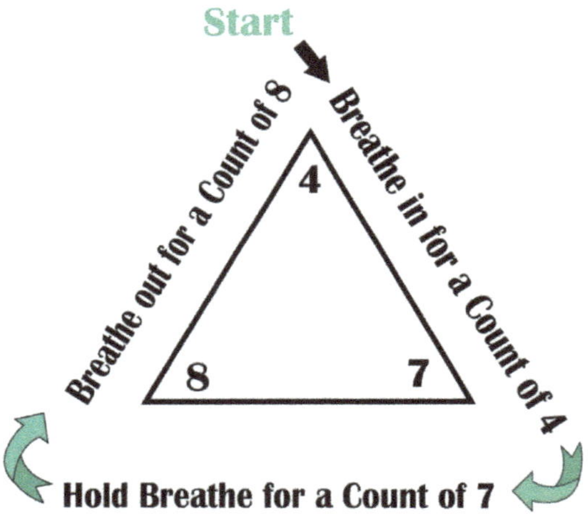

Sitting Positions and Stretches:

There are different sitting positions and stretches that can relax the body and release built-up tension. Hip stretches are known to release trapped emotions in the body because when the body is under stress, the psoas muscles (which are part of your hip flexors) tighten. When the stressful event is over, the tension and related emotions can remain trapped in the hips until it is released. See the diagrams below for stretches and sitting positions that are simple and easy to do.

Legs Up the Wall

Place your right hip flush against an available wall. (You will need to have enough space for your legs to comfortably rest against the wall.) Gently lean back and swing your legs up the wall. Your torso will draw a half-circle in space. The soles of your feet will be facing the ceiling with your legs extended and resting against the wall. You may not be able to maintain straight legs. If you have tight muscles, this will impact your ability to fully extend your legs. If this stretch is too intense, you may modify it by bending the knees and placing the soles of your feet against the wall. This is a great stretch to do before bed as it helps to slow down your heart rate. It's also great if you spend a lot of time on your feet throughout the day.

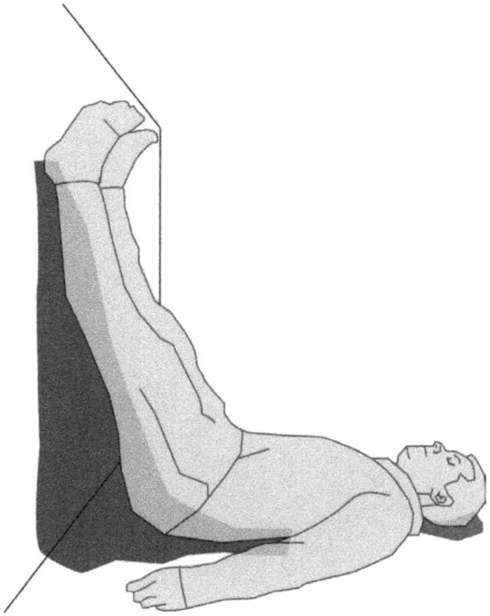

Easy Pose to Forward Fold

Find a comfortable seat on the ground. You may wish to sit on a pillow to elevate your hips. You may feel most comfortable with your legs folded or out in front of you. You may also want to use a rolled-up towel under your knees to help with any discomfort.

Inhale, and as you do, lengthen through your spine. You can imagine a string running from the base of your spine up until it reaches the center of your skull. Imagine someone is pulling this string to help you sit up tall.

Bring the shoulder blades back, spreading open the collarbone. Slide your ears back until there is a slight tuck in your chin. When you are ready, begin to move into the forward fold.

Forward Fold

Inhale a full breath, and as you exhale, begin to walk your hands down your legs or on the floor in front of you. Stop when you feel there is a good stretch without too much intensity. We are looking for a 6 out of 10, where 10 would be excruciating pain and 1 would be little to no sensation. You shouldn't experience any tingling, numbness, a need to hold your breath, frustration, or any other indicators you are experiencing pain.

If there is discomfort, simply walk your hands back until the intensity decreases. When you find your edge of sensation, stay in this pose for at least 20 seconds. You may have some rounding of the spine in order to fold over. You can work up to holding this for up to two minutes. Over time, you may be able to deepen the stretch and touch your toes.

You will get the most benefit from these poses if you are able to stay in them mindfully. This means not allowing your mind to wander to the future or past: what you had for breakfast or plans for meeting up with the guys after work.

You can stay in the present moment by counting your breath, noticing where you feel the stretch, listening to sounds in the room, noticing the temperature of the room, etc.

Hip Stretches:

From a seated position, bend your knees, placing the soles of your feet on the ground in front of you. Take your left ankle and place it on top of your right knee. You may place your hands on your shin for support.

Inhale to lift and lengthen through your spine, and as you exhale, bring your torso closer to the leg crossed in front of you. Hold for at least 20 seconds, remembering to come out at any time if it is too intense.

You may also try this without bending your knees from easy pose. From a crossed-legged seat, stack your left ankle on top of your right knee. Exhale to bend forward with a small rounding in your spine until you find a good level of intensity. Repeat on both sides, holding for at least 20 seconds.

Ball Under Foot Exercise

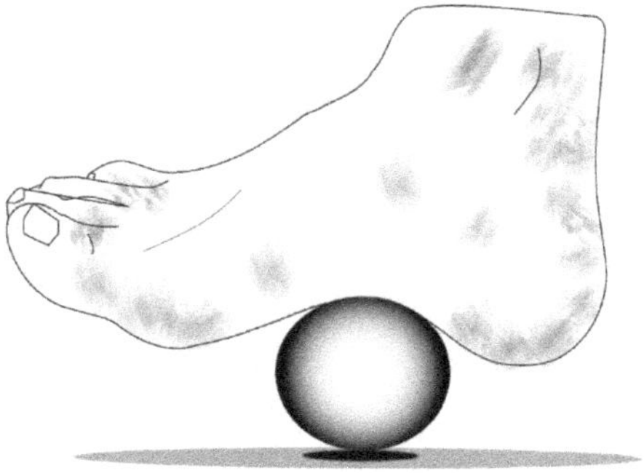

Place a tennis ball under one foot and stand on the other for balance. Slowly roll the ball underneath your foot and pay close attention to the physical sensations you feel as you roll the ball between your foot and the floor. Slowly apply increasing pressure with the weight of your body. Switch to the other foot and repeat.

Walking Meditation:

Remove your socks and shoes and walk throughout your home, noticing how different textures feel on your feet. Notice the cool tile or scratchy carpet. If the weather is appropriate and you are able, walk barefoot in dirt or grass. This is what is known as "earthing." Our bodies are basically conductors, so we can absorb free ions by connecting directly to the earth's surface. The ions act as antioxidants and have many health benefits.

Whole-Body Shaking:

When you are exposed to a stressful or traumatic event, your body goes into fight, flight, freeze, or faun. This is the activation of the stress cycle. The problem with this is that the human body does not naturally complete the stress cycle; it stores the emotions related to the traumatic event, causing damage and uncomfortable physical symptoms. You can bring the cycle to completion by shaking your whole body at once or by shaking one limb at a time. You can also achieve this through putting on music and dancing it out with your whole body.

Pendulum Self-Hug:

Infants in the womb are enclosed in a snug and comfortable space as they grow and develop. When their mothers move, they also move in a soothing, swaying motion.

Wrapping yourself tightly in a blanket (making sure you can still breathe easily) or hugging yourself as you sway in a pendulum motion can imitate this sensation and calm your body.

Humming, Singing, Gargling:

Since the Vagus nerve runs down past your nose and throat, it can be stimulated by humming, singing, or even gargling. Singing ten minutes per day can also lower depressive symptoms, so it's beneficial in more ways than one. We recommend singing alone in the car or shower or even joining a group.

Vibrational Breath:

Take a full breath in, and while exhaling, hum or say the word vuuuuu. Continue to do this until you feel grounded again.

Cold:

You can place an ice pack on your chest or back to stimulate the Vagus nerve. Rubbing an ice cube on your clavicle or taking a cold shower can also calm your body. In fact, an intense cold can lessen or even stop the duration of a panic attack.

Intense Cold:

This skill is taken from Dialectical and Behavioral Therapy (DBT) and is only appropriate for individuals with no cardiac issues. Be sure to speak with your physician before attempting to do so if you have any concerns.

You can place cold water (50+ degrees) in a large bowl. The bowl will need to be large enough to submerge your entire face. Hold your breath and place your face into the bowl for 30-60 seconds (Greene, 2022). Repeat until symptoms of panic have resolved. After completing this exercise, you may want to wrap up in a warm towel, blanket, or robe.

EFT Tapping:

EFT tapping is a stress-relief technique that combines acupressure and modern psychology. By tapping on specific points while focusing on distressing issues, it can reduce stress, lower cortisol, improve sleep, relieve pain, and boost well-being. It's simple, free, and easy to practice anywhere.

A 2012 study by Dr. Peta Stapleton, published in the *Journal of Nervous and Mental Disease*, found that EFT tapping significantly reduces cortisol levels compared to traditional talk therapy or resting. In a randomized, controlled trial, participants underwent 50 minutes of treatment, with cortisol measured before and after. The EFT tapping group experienced a 24% cortisol drop, while the talk therapy and no-treatment groups saw only a 14% reduction (*Science and Research*, 2020).

For more information, you can download Tapping Solutions, purchase books on EFT tapping, or visit the Tapping Solutions website: www.tappingsolutions.com.

HeartMath:

The heart and brain have a powerful two-way communication system, with the heart sending more signals to the brain than it receives. These signals influence emotional processing, memory, attention, and decision-making, with the heart actively affecting cognitive and emotional functioning. Research from the HeartMath Institute shows that emotional states impact heart activity. Negative emotions, like stress, create erratic heart rhythms that disrupt cognitive functions, impair decision-making, and reinforce the stress response. Conversely, positive emotions lead to stable heart rhythms that enhance mental clarity, emotional stability, and overall well-being.

Heart rate variability (HRV), the variation in heartbeats, is a key health indicator. High HRV reflects resilience, while low HRV is linked to stress and poor emotional regulation. By fostering positive emotions and improving heart rhythm coherence, individuals can enhance their mental, emotional, and physical health, highlighting the significant connection between heart and brain and the impact of emotional states on well-being.

You can purchase a sensor and app through the HeartMath website: www.heartmath.com

(*The Science of HeartMath - HeartMath*, 2024).

Neurofeedback:

Neurofeedback (NFB) is a brain training technique that uses physical and psychological noise to give the brain a reflection of itself, helping it adjust to a calmer, more focused state. Rather than suppressing emotions or creativity, it supports clients in overcoming obstacles to reach their full potential.

Infra-Low Frequency (ILF) neurofeedback targets brain waves. It is a safe, non-invasive, and non-verbal treatment that requires no effort from the client, making it accessible for all ages. This approach is particularly beneficial for those dealing with hypervigilance, emotional dysregulation, and stress. NFB is effective for conditions such as anxiety, PTSD, depression, ADD/ADHD, and traumatic brain injury (TBI) (*What Is ILF Neurofeedback? | the Neurofeedback Advocacy Project*, n.d.). To find out more, go to www.neuofeedbackadvocacyproject.com.

Touchpoint Solution:

Created over several decades by a team of neuropsychologists, TouchPoints utilize gentle, alternating vibrations to help reduce stress. They quickly shift your "fight-or-flight" response to a calmer, more balanced state, restoring a sense of control. Just place them on your body—in pockets, socks, straps, or wristbands—and experience relief in seconds (AdornThemes, n.d.).

www.thetouchpointsolution.com

Mindfulness:

Mindfulness is the practice of focusing on the present moment, a useful tool for alleviating anxiety by grounding oneself in the here and now. In times of stress, worry often centers around past regrets or future fears, which can amplify anxiety. Mindfulness counters this by promoting present-moment awareness, reinforcing a sense of safety and calm.

Renowned mindfulness expert John Kabat-Zinn describes mindfulness as "living in harmony with oneself and the world," encouraging people to connect deeply with each moment (Kabat-Zinn, 1994).

Key principles of mindfulness include:

1. Non-judging: Approach thoughts with curiosity rather than criticism, gently returning focus to the breath.
2. Patience: Allow time for quieting the mind, as patience can bring calm and support thoughtful responses in difficult moments.
3. Beginner's Mind: Embrace openness, stay curious, and be willing to let go of unhelpful habits.

4. Trust: Develop trust in your intuition and the gradual progress of your mindfulness journey.
5. Non-Striving: Avoid forcing outcomes; instead, experience life as it unfolds to manage challenges calmly.
6. Acceptance: Acknowledge your situation as it is, engaging openly with emotions and thoughts.
7. Letting Go: Release tension and expectations to make space for new experiences (Bastos, 2023).

Intrusive Thoughts and Negative Self-Talk:

Intrusive thoughts are the kind of thoughts that come into your mind when you do not want them to. They are often related to worry or fear and can be quite disturbing, especially if you tend to think, "I thought it, so it must be true." It's also important to know we have no control over the thoughts that come up, but we do have control over how we respond to them.

The brain is wired negatively for survival, which means we are more likely to experience negative thoughts. It's as if the negative and positive thoughts were a magnet for the brain. The negative thoughts stick, and the positive thoughts repel. This is so we are always on alert. If we can think of all the ways something can go wrong, we can prepare better, right? Perhaps, but there is a cost to this hypervigilance.

Unfortunately, as discussed earlier, this chronic worry is unhelpful in the long run. Many of us also experience negative self-talk, which are negative thoughts about ourselves that are hurtful or shameful. There are several techniques you can use for either or both kinds of negative thoughts. We have chosen thought diffusion and thought stopping to include in this chapter and have described both below.

Thought diffusion is a set of techniques created by Steven Hayes within his Acceptance and Commitment Therapy (ACT) model. These techniques help us remember that a thought is a thought and not always a reality. The exercises below will help you get some distance from your negative thoughts in order to avoid buying into them. In ACT, cognitive fusion refers to when our thoughts and verbal processes influence our behavior because we "fuse" with them (Batten, 2011). This is because we are giving our thoughts a lot of weight and power. This isn't necessarily always an issue. If I have the thought, "I need an onion for this recipe," I will see an onion in my mind in my vegetable crisper. I will then find the onion. Fusing with the thoughts around needing an onion isn't a big deal unless I didn't have an onion and decided to let it ruin my evening. Just remember, it's the negative thoughts, the unhelpful ones, we will most likely want to diffuse.

Repeating a word:

Pick a word, such as lemon or milk, and begin repeating it out loud. Stop when the word begins to lose meaning. This technique will remind you that thoughts are just thoughts. I can say I'm Oprah Winfrey out loud a million times, but it does not make it true, and after a million times, Oprah Winfrey will sound pretty funny.

The Jerk at the Party:

Think of your negative thoughts like an obnoxious neighbor who noticed you were having a party and invited himself over. He may follow you around, telling you how awful the food is or how much he hates your taste in music, but you don't have to give him any of your time or energy. If you decided to attempt to throw him out, it would cause a huge scene, resulting in embarrassment for everyone in attendance. Also, like our thoughts, it would do no good. You can't get this guy to leave; you are stuck with him. You also can't argue with him. He will always have an amazing rebuttal and a never-ending supply of energy. So, what do you do? You decide to deal with being uncomfortable and sit with him. You can even say to him, "Thanks for the information." Over time, he will realize you are pretty boring and begin to mingle with the other guests. You might still hear his obnoxious comments in the background, but they won't be as loud.

Silly Voice:

When you notice a thought arise, replay the thought in a silly voice. You can use a favorite cartoon character, an opera singer, or your least favorite politician. You can also practice singing aloud in an operatic style or with a fun accent. For example, you might imagine Mickey Mouse saying, "I am a complete idiot." Hearing these words in a silly or obnoxious way may help you snap out of it long enough to avoid fusing with thought. You can see how believing these negative thoughts could ruin your day and cause you to be less available mentally or emotionally to your partner (Sadurní Rodríguez, 2021).

Don't Engage the Bully:

Imagine you are on a bus. You are the driver. You also happen to have a few passengers on your bus. One passenger is an absolute pain in the ass. He tells you how awful you are throughout the day. The other passenger on your bus tends to tell you not to listen to these awful things and states why all these insults are lies. Although you may be tempted to turn around and tell Negative Ned to shut the hell up, this is counterproductive. Confronting these voices will only make them louder. You are going to ignore both passengers and not engage them in discussion. How? I implore you to simply state, "Thanks for the information," and move on. The above is an example of a non-engagement response (NER), which, simply put, is saying to the bully, "Maybe," instead of engaging in a debate.

NERs can be very effective in diffusing thoughts (International OCD Foundation, 2022).

Thought Stopping:

We have listed the four steps to this technique below:

1. **Notice** the thought but avoid any judgment about it. If you say something like, "That's a stupid thought" or "I shouldn't be thinking that," it will only make the thought stronger. Say to yourself instead, "I am having the thought that…"
2. **Challenge** the thought. Ask yourself, "Would someone I love say this thought is true?" or "What evidence do I have that this thought is true?"
3. **Dismiss** the thought with a visualization. You can picture a stop sign and say to yourself, "STOP!" You can picture the thought on a cloud or a train passing by. You can picture it written down on a piece of paper or as a Polaroid picture, shrinking smaller and smaller until it disappears. You can imagine painting over the thought with a roller or brush.
4. **Reframe** it with its opposite or something positive. Caveat: This positive cognition must be believable to

some degree. For example, "I'm so stupid" can be replaced with "I'm actually pretty smart." If you choose "I'm the smartest person alive!" it may not be helpful because you will quickly get lost in an internal debate about your level of intelligence. You can turn thoughts and worries about safety into "I'm okay" or "I'm relatively safe" (*4 Step Thought Blocking or Thought Stopping Technique*, n.d.).

Communication & How to Fight Fair

Personal Values (ACT):

Values work is a component of Acceptance and Commitment Therapy (ACT). Steven Hayes defines values as "intentional qualities of action that join together a string of moments into a meaningful path" (Hayes & Smith, 2005). He also states that "they help us make decisions, choose a direction for our lives, as well as find a sense of meaning or purpose" (Hayes S., 2020).

We hope that since you are reading this book, you value being able to communicate objectively with your partner in a patient, loving, and kind way. It is also helpful for you to understand that you and your partner may sometimes have differences in values regarding an issue or topic of concern. The consideration of each other's values can allow for compromise through mutual understanding.

We have listed over 40 values below to help you start thinking from a values perspective. We challenge you to begin checking in with your personal values daily. How are you ensuring you are in line with them? What needs to change? If nothing needs to change, what is one small step you can take to pivot yourself toward them?

List of Values:

Acceptance
Adventure
Authenticity
Assertiveness
Care/Self-care
Compassion/Self-compassion
Cooperation
Courage
Creativity
Curiosity
Encouragement
Excitement
Fairness
Fitness
Flexibility
Freedom/Independence
Friendliness
Forgiveness
Fun & Humor

Gratitude
Honesty
Integrity
Industry
Intimacy
Kindness
Love
Mindfulness
Order/Organization
Persistence
Pleasure
Respect
Responsibility
Safety/Protection
Sexuality
Skillfulness
Support
Trust (Collis, 2022)

How to Fight Fair:

Below is a list of our favorite tools for managing conflict. We have provided information on effective communication, strategies for managing intense conversations, and information on why we fight unfairly and what to do about it.

Nonviolent Communication:

Nonviolent Communication (NVC) is a formula and way of communicating created by psychologist Marshall Rosenberg. In his book *Nonviolent Communication,* he explains how he helped leaders of countries at war sit down and speak with one another using NVC. This form of communication is a great place to start to manage conflict with your partner. It also helps us avoid old patterns of defensiveness, stonewalling, criticism, and contempt, a.k.a. The Four Horsemen of the Apocalypse.

The NVC formula:

1. When you____________: Insert something your partner did. This must be a fact. There is no room for assumptions or judgment here.
   Example: When you walked away and slammed the door…

2. I felt__________: Insert *emotion* here. Again, *only* an emotion. No judgments.
   Example: I felt hurt, scared, angry, and sad. Avoid words like disrespected or ridiculed, which insinuates your partner has a character flaw.

3. I need ________: Insert your need here.

Example: I need to know I am safe. I need to know you love me. I would like us to compromise on our budget, etc.

4. Would you be willing to ________: Insert action you would like from your partner. This cannot be a demand. This is ONLY a request. Your partner can say no because, remember, you cannot control people. Example: Would you be willing to see a couples counselor to learn how to work together as a team? Would you be willing to meet with a financial planner?

The complete formula:

When you______, I felt_____. I need ______. Would you be willing to____? (Rosenberg, M., 2015).

There are workshops and workbooks on learning and practicing NVC if you would like to explore this topic further. I suggest you write down a few of the typical issues you and your partner struggle with and fill out the formula above when calm and collected. This way, you will already have an idea of how to respond in a respectful and kind manner.

Self-compassion & Taking a Time-out:

Dr. Kristen Neff is a self-compassion guru. Research shows that self-compassion is actually more impactful and healthier than self-esteem. She has broken down self-compassion into three components:

1. **Self-kindness:** This means treating ourselves with empathy and patience. Giving ourselves support instead of criticism. I often encourage my clients to give themselves a hug when things are hard or to say to themselves, "This is hard." Remember to talk to yourself like you would a good buddy. If he was having a rough day, you wouldn't call him an idiot or ridicule him because you know that wouldn't be helpful. It's the same with how we talk to ourselves. Criticism isn't helpful.
2. **Common humanity:** This is a reminder we are all human. We all make mistakes. None of us are perfect. Also, this is a reminder that suffering is a human experience. We all suffer. You are not alone.
3. **Mindfulness:** This component of self-compassion is a reminder to observe our suffering with acceptance. We avoid suppressing our suffering or exaggerating it. Again, if a friend sat on your couch and complained about losing out on a promotion at work, what would you do? You certainly wouldn't dismiss him, and you wouldn't tell him to give up because losing the promotion was the end of the world. You can validate your struggles without letting them cripple you (Self-compassion, 2024).

Self-compassion is a good approach to take when struggling with our partner. You may need to take a time-out when in conflict to offer yourself some self-compassion. I encourage you to share this with your partner so you both can stay objective and not let emotions take over.

Time Out:

It's important to come up with a phrase or word when in conflict with our partner. This is so you both are aware when the other is in danger of saying or doing something they will regret later. Here are a few suggestions or examples of phrases you could use:

"Time out."
"Let's take a breather."
"Let's take ten."
"I need to breathe."
"I need time."
"Red alert."

Feel free to come up with your own phrase if none of these feel right. It can even be something silly. Get creative! Laughter is a quick coping skill that allows us to get out of our fight-or-flight response. Make sure you inform your partner of this phrase and that he/she is aware this time and space request is not negotiable. Time out means time out. It does not mean you are abandoning each other.

It does not mean you no longer care for your partner. It does not mean you are avoiding talking about something difficult.

Make sure you come up with a time to revisit the discussion when you are both back to baseline. Set and setting are very important. Remember your inner toddler? Make sure you have eaten, gotten enough sleep, are sober, etc., before you resume or bring up the topic of concern. Make sure you have privacy and enough time set aside. Don't try to have a tough conversation ten minutes before you need to leave for work. I suggest requesting time from your partner to ensure you are both prepared.

The second piece of a time-out is remembering to pay attention to the cues that will let you know you are heading into the danger zone. This is when you feel overwhelmed, overstimulated, or defensive. You can go back to Chapter 5 to review triggers, emotions, and body sensations to help you decipher this. Dr. John Gottman has one strategy for this that he discusses in his book *The Seven Principles for Making Marriage Work*. He suggests purchasing a heart rate monitor you can wear around your wrist. When your heart rate is above 100 beats per minute (80 if you are an athlete), you will know you are too activated to speak from a logical place. When we get angry, we can no longer hear our partner, nor can we think or speak effectively. Your partner might as well be trying to have a discussion with a crazed orangutan. There really is no point in trying to have a discussion from this level of activation. Take a twenty-minute break to allow yourself to get back in the right headspace (Gottman J.M, & Silver, N., 2015). Now, let's review another important concept by the world-renowned marriage and family therapist John Gottman: The Four Horsemen of the Apocalypse.

The Four Horsemen of The Apocalypse:

As we touched lightly on this in the introduction, we will now explain the importance of the Four Horsemen. This is a metaphor for the toxic ways in which we can treat our partners that will often lead to break up or divorce. Dr. Gottman, PhD., named these the Four Horsemen of the Apocalypse. Gottman states that he can identify with 90% accuracy whether a couple will stay together based on whether the Four Horsemen are present within a relationship.

The Four Horsemen Antidotes

Criticism: Using harshness, blaming, judgment, or disapproval when dealing with a conflict.	**Gentle Startup:** Approaching in a gentle way, focusing on the problem and not your partner. Using "I feel" statements.
Defensiveness: Refusing to take responsibility for your own actions, shifting blame.	**Take Responsibility:** Being accountable and apologizing sincerely.
Contempt: Showing anger, hostility, or disgust toward your partner. Name-calling.	**Share Fondness and Admiration:** Showing your partner love and admiration regularly. Giving compliments, affection, and encouragement.
Stonewalling: Shutting down emotionally or withdrawing during an important discussion or conflict.	**Self-soothing:** Using somatic exercises such as deep breathing or grounding to stay calm and present for your partner.

Although none of these horsemen are ideal for relationships, some couples have all four present and can still remain together. The research shows that this is because these couples are able to repair well (Gottman J.M, & Silver, N., 2015). Repair means being able to apologize with authenticity and make efforts and requests for reconnection. Repair can happen in many ways, but only if your partner is open to it.

Repair can be respecting your partner's request for time and space before attempting an apology. Sometimes we aren't ready to hear an in-depth apology right after an argument, and that's okay. Repair can be a change in behavior. Repair can be a long hug or a well-timed joke. Again, the important piece to remember is to make sure you take the time and effort to repair and reconnect. You may need to apologize and ask your partner *how* you can make it better. Your partner may have a preferred way of repair. Take the time to ask and find out what that is. I suggest you continue to ask after an argument to ensure effective repair is happening. If you agree to change a behavior, follow through with that change. If you go back to old habits and old patterns, your partner will lose faith in you.

Obviously, that isn't great for the longevity of the relationship.

ACT with Love

ACT with Love, written by Russ Harris, uses components of Acceptance and Commitment Therapy (ACT) to help us have happy, healthy relationships. There are a few take-aways from this book I often tell clients who are struggling in their relationships. Here they are:

Relationship Myths

1. **The Perfect Partner**
   Expecting a perfect partner leads to disappointment. Growth and self-improvement are essential, but perfection isn't realistic. Everyone has flaws—we're all human.

2. **A Partner Will Complete Me**
   No single person can fulfill all our needs. Relying solely on a partner creates dependency and fear of abandonment. Instead, we benefit from connections with multiple people in different roles, creating a well-rounded support system

3. **Love is Easy**
   Even with someone very similar, relationships involve disagreements. Love, like life, has ups and downs. Conflict isn't avoidable but can be managed healthily.

4. **Everlasting Love is a Feeling**
   Love isn't a constant feeling; it's an ongoing action. While loving feelings may come and go, true commitment means choosing to act with love even when emotions fluctuate.

Stop Telling the Story

When we're upset with our partner, it's easy to fall into a "story" of negative thoughts: "They always…" "They never…" This narrative causes us to recall every past mistake, escalating our frustration and casting our partner in an unfairly negative light. Relationship expert Esther Perell discusses this in her YouTube video, *Stop Bickering: It's Killing Your Relationship*. She explains that a more effective approach is listening for an unmet need or asking for a need to be met. For example: "You never do the dishes" vs. "I've had a long day. I'm exhausted. Would you mind doing the dishes?" (Esther Perel, 2017).

Our brains naturally focus on the negative, especially in conflict. Unless there's genuine harm happening, we need to let go of this story. Recognize it as just that—a story, not the full picture of who your partner is. This mindset helps you stay fair and open, making it easier to move forward together.

I'm Right, You're Wrong

This is another form of storytelling. If you focus on who is right and who is wrong, you inevitably put up a wall between you and your partner. There is no room for compromise, teamwork, or connection (Harris, R., 2009).

Right or wrong is subjective and can spark an hour - to days-long stalemate. Anyone on the high school debate team can tell you any side of an argument can be defended. The only exception here is abuse. If abuse is happening, the abuser is the one at fault. End of story.

The Red Flags of Abuse

I would like to briefly define abuse to help you acknowledge if it is present in your relationship. If the list below at all reflects your relationship, additional support will be needed to heal. There are many domestic violence organizations for victim support, as well as clinicians who specialize in this area. Please reach out to your local organizations for support if needed. There is no shame in asking for help; you are not alone.

You may be surprised to find out there are several different types of abuse. Emotional, verbal, physical, sexual, financial, and psychological. Abuse is a set of repeated behaviors utilized in order to control someone. It typically stems from a fear of abandonment and a deep belief system around hierarchy. Abusive partners believe their partners belong to them. Sometimes, this personal belief is so deeply ingrained that the perpetrator may not be fully aware of it. This seed is planted because of what was modeled to them on how to have a relationship and how to treat a partner. If you are abusing your partner, you will need a trained professional to help you address and change unhealthy beliefs.

- **Emotional Abuse**
  Humiliation, ridicule, manipulation, ignoring partner, threatening to leave your partner.

- **Physical Abuse**
  Any physical contact done in order to inflict pain or damage, standing too close, or threatening to cause physical harm.

- **Verbal Abuse**
  Insulting partner, using derogatory language, or yelling.

- **Sexual Abuse**
  Any sexual interaction (touching, fondling, intercourse, penetration, oral sex, etc.) without consent. Certain individuals cannot give full consent, including children, intoxicated individuals, if one is not fully awake, as well as individuals with cognitive delay or deficits.

The Components of Sexual Consent:

- Clear information is given, continuously discussed, and consent is freely given without coercion
- Consent can change from moment to moment
- Should be given with enthusiasm and excitement

(*What Consent Looks Like | Helping Survivors of Sexual Assault and Abuse*, 2024)

- **Financial Abuse**
  Controlling a partner's ability to work, threatening to withdraw financial support, hindering the ability to make financial decisions, or have access to funds. This could be disabling the car right before a shift begins, ensuring the partner will be fired, or destroying property requiring new items to be purchased. This could be locking a partner in the home or showing up to a place of work to humiliate a partner in front of coworkers. Some abusive partners require a partner to ask permission any time they ask for access to their own money and interrogate them about how the money will be spent. Uncontrollable spending to damage a partner's credit or put them in a bad situation due to financial difficulty.

- **Psychological Abuse**
  Questioning a partner's reality as well as challenging their reality. Using their partner's mental illness against them. Examples: "You are just being crazy." "You are just a dumb drunk." "You are SO dramatic." "Get a hold of yourself."

Minimizing a partner's feelings and denying they said or did something to hurt you. Lying to a partner when concerns are brought up. Hiding something a partner is looking for only to put it out in plain sight in order to make a partner feel they are going crazy.

Some Advice from the Authors:

Pick Your Battles

Couples have differing thoughts, opinions, values, perspectives, and life experiences. This means we are bound to find things to argue about. However, if you fought about everything that makes you different, you would spend too much time and energy waging a never-ending war. If you have a concern to bring to the table, make sure it is worth the upset it will cause. We tend to cause a level of hurt even when we are completely justified in bringing up the issue. My advice is to pick your battles. You can't fight them all, and you certainly won't win them all. Too many fights can lead a partner to feel they can't win or will never be "good enough" for you.

Give Your Partner the Benefit of the Doubt:

This is another way to address negative thoughts, feelings, and judgments of our partner. Reframe negative thoughts about your partner with positive ones. Instead of thinking, "She's such a nag," reframe it with, "She must be feeling overwhelmed and needs my help." Trusting your partner's actions and behaviors are coming from good intentions, a misunderstanding, or other viewpoints will foster positive feelings such as empathy and compassion.

Needs & Intent:

Before you get defensive with your partner, try to listen for the need and intention. What are they hoping to accomplish by bringing up this issue? What is the need? We have listed human needs below to help you respond to conflict with positive actions vs. unhelpful ones. Once you identify the need, it may simply be asking your partner how you can fulfill the need.

CONNECTION
acceptance
affection
appreciation
belonging
cooperation
communication
closeness
community
companionship
compassion
consideration
consistency
empathy
inclusion
intimacy
love
mutuality

nurturing
respect/self-respect
safety
security
stability
support
to know and be known
to see and be seen
to understand and be understood
trust
warmth

PHYSICAL WELL-BEING
air
food
movement/exercise
rest/sleep
sexual expression
safety
shelter
touch
water

HONESTY
authenticity
integrity
presence

PLAY
joy
humor

PEACE
beauty
communion
ease
equality
harmony
inspiration
order

AUTONOMY
choice
freedom
independence
space
spontaneity

MEANING
awareness
celebration of life
challenge
clarity
competence
consciousness

contribution
creativity
discovery
efficacy
effectiveness
growth
hope
learning
mourning
participation
purpose
self-expression
stimulation
to matter
understanding

(Fizyta & Center for Nonviolent Communication, 2005)

The Trifecta: Exercise, Sleep and Diet

It is well-known among mental health providers that you cannot have optimal mental health if you are not taking care of your physical health. This includes three important factors: exercise, sleep, and diet. What most people do not realize is that the reverse is also true: If you are not taking good care of your mental health, your physical health will also suffer. This is because everything in our bodies is connected, so each system affects the other, and that includes mental and emotional states.

Regular exercise is something that we routinely recommend to our clients because it is so effective in improving mental health outcomes. Sharma et al. (2006) state, "Exercise improves mental health by reducing anxiety, depression, and negative mood by improving self-esteem and cognitive function. Exercise has also been found to alleviate symptoms such as low self-esteem and social withdrawal." If you do not have a regular exercise regimen, we recommend you start one. You can begin with something as simple as walking or joining a local gym. Moving your body for at least 20 minutes a day in a way that feels good is a great place to start.

We also emphasize to clients that sleep is crucial for good mental health and that lack of sleep can exacerbate or even cause mental illness. A 2021 article published in The Sleep Medical Reviews academic journal states that "poor sleep has also been associated with post-traumatic stress, eating disorders, and psychosis spectrum experiences such as delusions and hallucinations. Studies have also found that specific sleep disorders, such as sleep apnea, circadian rhythm disruption, restless leg syndrome, excessive daytime sleepiness and narcolepsy, sleepwalking, and nightmares are all more prevalent in those experiencing mental health difficulties."

Nutritional psychiatry is a new and rapidly emerging field of study that focuses on the gut–brain connection in the body and how it affects mental health. Diet affects the gut biomes, so it should be considered when a person is suffering from mental health conditions, such as anxiety or depression. Americans typically consume foods that are high in fat and sugar and are processed. Owen and Corfe (2014) state, "Both cross-sectional and longitudinal studies have shown that the more one eats a Western or highly processed diet, the more one is at risk for developing psychiatric symptoms, such as depression and anxiety."

For further tools and resources, head to the suggested reading/resource section of the back of the book! In the next chapter, we will begin to add strategies and tips to your toolbox for taking on more of the emotional labor in your relationship. We will also help you balance the mental load within your relationship so both partners feel supported and valuable members of the team. Good luck! We are rooting for you!

NOTES :

CHAPTER 7:

How To Love The 21st-Century Woman (by Stacy)

It's Mother's Day, and I am enjoying the luxury of sleeping in late when I wake to my youngest, Cora, climbing into my bed with me. She tells me excitedly about the trip to the play place her dad has planned for her and her twin brothers that day. I sit up groggily, and she proudly hands me a box of my favorite Belgian chocolates. There are also handmade gifts from all three of my kids to open and a new summer dress from my husband.

I know I have the option of doing pretty much whatever I want to on "my day." Unfortunately, the guilt I feel at being idle continues to nag at me throughout the day, so I help out with the kids and finish sanding the varnish off the bathroom vanity as part of our ongoing home renovations.

The day ends with me taking my daughter to the park while my husband, Eric, puts burgers on the grill.

When I asked Eric the day before if we had any plans for Mother's Day, he said he never plans anything on the actual day, "because of how crazy it gets out there," meaning all the popular brunch spots or spas I might have wanted to visit would be packed. We typically celebrate Valentine's Day after the fact as well. I'd rather talk to a car salesman from the dentist's chair while having a root canal than go to a restaurant on Valentine's Day.

Eric didn't ask me what I'd like to do for Mother's Day this year, which he typically does. Upon reflection, I think I know why he didn't ask—a few days before, I had shared with him my thoughts on a recent post from one of my favorite social media relationship gurus, Zac Watson. Zac Watson, #RecoveringManChild, coaches men on emotional labor and the mental load. I have been following him online for about a year now, and I feel that the content of his videos is exactly what we are attempting to address in this book. Zac provides education, ideas, and recommendations for taking on more emotional labor and reducing the mental load for our partners.

He recently posted a video preparing men for Mother's Day. In this video, he suggested giving the mothers of their children options for how they could celebrate Mother's

Day. He strongly discouraged men from asking, "Hey, honey, what would you like to do for Mother's Day?" You may be wondering why, and I will explain in detail in this chapter, along with several other important concepts discussed in Zac's video. I encourage you to look him up and begin watching his videos in addition to what you are reading here. You also have the option of reaching out to him for personal coaching if you choose.

Expect Resistance

There will be days when you feel like giving up. There will be moments when you think, "I have done everything possible to please her, but she's still complaining!" How do I know this? Because Eric and I went through this at the beginning of our relationship and continue to navigate this feeling of frustration at times. Within my own research, I have noticed a few common responses from women who have a partner who is attempting to help. I have compiled a list of these responses below so you can plan and avoid some of these pitfalls.

A Lack of Trust

At first, your partner may not yet fully trust you to take over some of the tasks on the to-do list. She may believe it will be faster and done more effectively if she takes care of it herself. Which, in all honesty, might be correct. After all, these are things she has thought about, planned, and executed many times. As a child, she probably played house with her friends in her pretend kitchen or made mud pies in the backyard. She may have watched many of the women in her family doing household tasks and received detailed instructions on how to do them. I remember my grandmother showing me how to make a bed when I was probably six or seven years old. Give yourself some grace when you stumble or don't get it right the first time. Practice makes perfect, right? Also, you may have to advocate for yourself here by asking her to let you try and fail a few times before you get it right.

Fear of Being Viewed as a Failure

Your partner may be afraid to tell you exactly what she needs help with and how she would like it done. Why? Because women have been socialized to believe that a large part of their worth is based on maintaining a household. Simply put, asking for help means I'm failing as a woman and I'm not a valuable member of society. When a partner suddenly suggests taking some of the emotional labor and mental load from her, it may be scary for her. It may even cause a level of guilt or shame within her. She may get angry and assume you are criticizing her by offering to help. Let her know you want to help so she has more time and space for the things that bring her joy.

This message of value based on domesticity may even be a message other woman around her are perpetuating. For example, saying such things as "You are so lucky to have a husband who helps with the kids." In some cultures, this belief is deeply ingrained in the family system. You will need to support her through maintaining healthy boundaries with family and friends. Perhaps you respond by saying, "I'm only doing my share of the work. No more, no less. We are a team."

Fear of You

She may be avoiding an argument because of how you have responded to requests for support in the past. Maybe you were mean or rude about her asking because you had to stop doing something you were enjoying. Here is where I suggest you *never* tell your wife to stop "nagging" you. The word 'nag' has become a sexually demeaning word. It's right up there with calling her a bitch or a whore. It's a horrible word used too easily to put women down. It's a low blow. Go back and read Chapters 5-7 if you need tips and reminders for effective communication and managing negative emotions. You will have to learn to respond to her requests for help with a level of enthusiasm. Remember, you are showing her your love through these tasks, which is an important component of intimacy and connection.

Fear of Disappointment or Extra Work

Women are trying to "have it all," so to speak. Many women want careers, children, a loving partner, adventure, self-fulfillment, etc. As we have discussed before, all these expectations are impossible for one person to manage. Women are used to feeling like failures. Many of us also believe no one else will do the work if we don't. If we ask for help, we fear it won't be done "right," and we will just have to do the task again.

When a partner offers to complete a task and does it in a sloppy, rushed way, it can result in feelings of hurt and disappointment. It can send the message that "this isn't important to me, so I'm not going to give it much effort or thought." I genuinely believe most men aren't even aware of this thought. They go through the motions of helping out their partners (although reluctantly), assuming the task was done "good enough."

I have experienced this myself. One year at Christmas, Eric and I visited family in Minnesota for the holidays. We often have a big family gathering with food, gift-giving, and socializing. I love to cook and decided to prepare several dishes to add to the holiday meal. After spending hours in the kitchen, I was on to my last and final treat: a batch of chocolate chip cookies. I asked Eric to help me scoop out the dough, roll it into balls, and add it to the cookie sheet so I could take a break. I returned to the kitchen ten minutes later to check on his progress. The first few rows of cookies were done perfectly. I then noticed the last two rows. They looked awful. I could immediately see what he had done—he had scooped out a lump of dough and squeezed it instead of rolling it. They didn't look appetizing due to the obvious imprint of his fingers in the dough. I don't know about you, but I don't want to eat a cookie that looks like someone's hand was in it. We laugh about this today, but I still feel a little hurt when I think about it. The message here is that if you agree to take on a task, do it with tender, loving care (TLC). Especially if it's cooking. Food just tastes better when it's prepared with love.

You may be wondering how you will know if a job is done correctly or to your partner's standards. I'm going to use an example here to help you understand what most women expect when they say "clean and tidy." You know how much I love examples! (It's a therapist thing.)

If you go to a bank to fill out a loan application with a loan officer, what do you expect the lobby to look like? What will your loan officer's desk look like? If there was an overflowing garbage can attracting flies in the lobby, would you notice? Would you notice empty sucker wrappers on the floor from the many toddlers visiting the bank? Would you feel uneasy if your loan officer had empty food containers on her desk left over from a few days of lunch? How about stacks of random paperwork everywhere? Another point to consider is what you expect when you stay in a hotel. Would you notice if the sheets were rumpled and the bed unmade? Would you notice dirty towels on the bathroom floor? An empty toilet paper holder? You have standards outside of your home, so why would you not have these same standards within your home?

Start thinking about your house as a place where you have standards but also allow an agreed-upon level of mess. No one wants to feel like they are living in a museum *or* a junkyard. I also want to make sure to mention that if your partner tends to be on the messy side, this may be because she is overwhelmed and burnt out. With your help, this may motivate her to adopt a higher standard when she notices half of her to-do list has been removed permanently by you.

If you decide to hire someone to clean once a week, this will not be enough to maintain most women's standard level of neatness. Also, you will need to do the emotional labor and mental load required to make that happen. This includes finding and hiring the person, scheduling the time for them to show up, and arranging payment. You will also make sure the floors and counters are clear before the cleaner arrives so clutter won't get in the way. Don't try to put all this on your partner, stating, "I'm paying for it, so you have to make the arrangements." Some women would rather pocket the cash and do the cleaning themselves to avoid having to manage everything that goes into hiring and maintaining a cleaner. You might be thinking you have found an easy solution to this problem, but you must include what goes into making this happen. Otherwise, you run the risk of adding more to your partner's plate, not less.

If you have a partner who is terrified of germs, spends hours focusing on one domestic task but cannot seem to complete it, and will not allow anyone else to help, this may indicate a need for support from an outside professional. A mental health professional who treats Obsessive Compulsive Disorder (OCD) or Obsessive Compulsive Personality Disorder (OCPD) may be necessary. If you have a partner who will not throw anything away, they may need assistance from someone specializing in treating individuals who struggle with hoarding. You can find more information about these conditions and where to find help on the International Obsessive Compulsive Disorder Foundation's (IOCDF) website. More on this will be provided in the resource section at the back of the book.

Fear of Lost Time

As we discussed at the beginning of the book, asking a partner to give instructions on how to complete household tasks only adds to the mental load. Avoid asking how to do something, where something is located, or interrupting your partner to ask these questions. These attempts to help, although well intended, will only put more responsibility on your partner's shoulders. Remember, the path to hell is paved with good intentions! Do your best to complete the task, even if it takes you longer to look for something in the house or look up the information needed. Don't ask your partner how much teething medication to give the baby; look at the back of the bottle or call the pediatrician's office. Don't ask where the diaper cream is. Look on the changing table and in the diaper bag. You got this!

If you are the type of guy who tries to find a better, faster way of completing a task, I recommend putting this mentality on hold for now. Once you have built trust with your partner, she may be willing to discuss change and compromise. Some of the items you will be taking on will be new to you. It may be as simple as folding towels, which she has done a million times and has a system. She knows how to fold them so they will *all* fit in the closet. So don't assume she's just being anal-retentive.

Be Consistent & Follow Through

If you tell your partner you will take on feeding and watering the dog each morning, do not let anything get in the way of that commitment. The moment you forget and she ends up doing your agreed-upon job, you have slid back down the trust mountain ten thousand feet. You will have to start over, and it's only going to get steeper with each slip. This isn't to say women won't experience their own hurdles and stumbles throughout this journey.

I have heard stories of women leaving the dishes in the sink as an experiment to see when their partner will notice them, only to be stuck with a smelly sink of dishes several days later. This usually results in an angry outburst at a partner for not noticing. Maybe he will apologize and load the dishwasher that night, but over time, the dishes will default again to her.

A friend of mine put her husband's clean laundry on his side of the bed under the comforter. When he tried to climb into bed that night, he realized his laundry was in the way. Although I found this to be a funny story, these passive-aggressive tactics won't get you anywhere in the long run. Women need to be vulnerable, ask for help, and then stand back and receive the help. Men need to follow through and be consistent.

The Nuts & Bolts of Managing Emotional Labor and the Mental Load

Now that we have discussed common obstacles of taking on emotional labor and how to manage these barriers, let's get into the logistics of executing emotional and mental labor.

1. Observe. Take Notes. Investigate:

I recommend observing your partner and what she is doing throughout the day over the next couple of days. Make sure this includes a Saturday or Sunday so you get the full picture. This doesn't mean following her around and interrogating her. Just be curious, like a scientist observing a newly discovered exotic bird. Isn't she lovely? Take notes. Ask about her day and listen for the emotional labor she completed. Remember, emotional labor is any task she is doing to maintain a connection with the people in her life. This often includes managing others' emotions, feelings, and needs at the expense of her own. This could be as simple as listening to your worries about a meeting with your boss at work today or helping your daughter pick out her favorite outfit for picture day at school. Also, take note of the mental load she is managing and how long tasks take to complete. How long did it take her to fill out the school photo order form and get your daughter dressed, in the car, and safely delivered to school?

If you notice times when she is attempting to complete a task and is interrupted, add a star to the task. This will remind you that this task was made more difficult by the interruption. Executive functioning skills involve memory, planning, prioritizing, task initiation, impulse control, emotional control, and cognitive flexibility. The mental load involves the executive functioning skills your partner is employing to manage the never-ending to-do list.

2. Express Gratitude:

Now that you have a list of what emotional labor and the mental load look like for your partner, start thanking her. You do not have to say thank you for everything she does in exhaustive detail. A few descriptive details are enough. For example, "Thanks for washing and drying my gym shorts." "Thanks for picking up our son's favorite cereal. I know this helped us avoid a crazy morning." Pick a few things throughout the day to thank her for. I hope by now you have naturally increased the amount of gratitude you feel for your partner, and your expressed appreciation will be genuine. Avoid making broad statements such as, "Babe, you are superwoman. Thanks for everything you do." My father used to say women are goddesses. I didn't fully understand why this statement always irritated me. Now, I understand that giving these compliments is not only vague but highlights how much is expected of us. It also sends the message we shouldn't complain because our superpowers are being acknowledged. If I'm *not* juggling everything, what does this say about me? Am I the opposite of a superhero? It's asking a lot of our partners to wear a cape, and it's an unrealistic standard to meet.

3. Take Inventory:

In order to avoid adding more to your partner's mental load, resist asking her where items are in the house, what is needed for an activity, or the dreaded "What's for dinner?" Take some time going through closets, drawers, the refrigerator, etc., and take a basic inventory. Write the items down in your notebook. This will help you avoid interrupting your partner and adding to her mental load. Don't forget to look underneath and behind things. Don't ask your wife where something is unless you have spent a good amount of time and effort looking for it on your own. The goal is to minimize the times you ask where something is as much as possible. It seems like a simple thing, but it can be extremely frustrating for a partner.

Take notice if your family's staples are getting low, and add them to the grocery list. If you notice the ketchup bottle is half full, add it to the grocery list. These small things can have a huge impact on how your partner perceives you. If you are already doing some of these things, bravo! Keep it up!

4. Divide and Conquer:

You will need to decide who will do what as far as emotional labor goes in your home, as well as how, what, where, and when. I have some fabulous news for you. Eve Rodsky, the author of *Fair Play*, did intensive labor and research to create a system for dividing emotional labor. She also created a companion deck of cards to make this even simpler. You can pick up a copy of the book and read it with your partner or purchase the deck of cards. I highly recommend both. However, if you choose to sit down with your partner and do this on your own, make sure to include the below components:

- Schedule a time when you are both calm, cool, and collected. Give yourself at least an hour to create the first draft so you don't feel rushed.
- Decide if there are any tasks that do not fall in line with your personal values as a couple. Are you sending Christmas cards to everyone you know, even to people you rarely see or interact with? Perhaps this is something you could decide to take off the list. This task includes personal values around time and money, and it may not be in line with what matters the most to you. This also may require some compromise if you disagree with your partner on this issue.
- Discuss what each item on the to-do list requires from start to finish in order to be considered complete. Don't forget to calculate the time it will take to complete the task.
- Be realistic about the time frame. If you have offered to take on packing for trips, don't wait until the morning before the flight to throw everything in a suitcase. Some items will need to be done daily or every few days, such as dishes or laundry.
- Be fair. Make sure you are taking as close to equal the number of tasks as possible, especially the daily tasks

that are time-consuming. This includes things like cooking dinner or packing lunches.

- If life events occur for your partner, such as the loss of a job or death in the family, you may need to take on more until your partner is in a more stable place emotionally.
- Explore items on the list and consider the standard level of care or cleanliness. A standard level of care would be to ensure your child brushes their teeth before bed or assist them with homework until it is completed.
- Employing a financial adviser, nanny, or other professional to assist with the emotional labor *creates* emotional labor. Make sure to consider this when choosing this option.
- Prepare for change. The emotional labor happening in the home will change over time. Make sure to have regular discussions to ensure you are keeping up with change. This may look like figuring out transportation to a new dance class your daughter has joined or giving away the clothes she no longer fits in. If you are going through a kitchen renovation, your dish duty may turn into ordering food and ensuring you have paper plates, etc. I recommend the biodegradable options.
- Change or swap tasks to avoid burnout. Your partner may prefer to take on laundry instead of dishes after a few months.

- Commit to not giving up. As tempting as it might be, don't give up. We recognize this will be a huge shift for some of our readers, but we believe in you. There will be challenges in this journey, but it's usually the difficult obstacles that lead to the most rewards.
- Don't go back to old habits, and don't embrace rigidity. "This is just who I am, and my partner needs to accept me as is." That last statement has broken up two marriages recently within my own family. Refusing to change and grow isn't a worthy hill to die on. Human beings change, despite what these men in my family believe. You're not the same person you were in fifth grade, are you? No. You are older and wiser. You will continue to grow emotionally, mentally, and spiritually if you can embrace flexibility.

When things are frustrating beyond belief and you want to give up, remember your partner is struggling too. When we remember this, we can extend a little more patience and grace to our loved ones. We hope you feel excited to start this journey and hopeful about what the future will bring.

NOTES :

CHAPTER 8:
Boundaries & The Couple Bubble (by Stacy)

Boundaries

You may be wondering what a boundary is. Our personal boundaries are rules and limits we set with ourselves and others in order to ensure our relationships are healthy. They protect us from abuse *from* others and resentment *toward* others. Boundaries also ensure we don't betray ourselves by allowing ourselves to be a doormat. Boundary setting is a vital part of the work I do with my clients. Everyone needs boundaries! Why? Well, when we don't have healthy boundaries, we build resentment toward the people in our lives. As we have discussed at the beginning of this book, resentment is a relationship killer. Saying yes out of obligation, fear of push-back, or rejection leads to resentment. We get tired of being hurt and putting ourselves last. Anger can often show up when a boundary has been crossed. If you find yourself feeling angry with someone in your life, you may need to consider if a boundary crossing has occurred and how to address it.

If you have no idea what I'm talking about, answer these questions. Have you ever agreed to help a buddy move on a weekend when you were already overbooked? Maybe you said yes because in the past, he's bullied you until you agreed. How did you feel after helping him? What if your buddy never seemed to be available when you asked for *his* help? What if you threw out your already bad back by lifting his couch? As you think this scenario through, do you notice feelings of anger, irritation, or frustration? Bingo! This is the beginning of resentment building within this friendship. If this type of interaction is common with this amigo, the relationship is in danger. You may start to avoid him, and eventually, with time and distance, the friendship will be no more. Ironically, the more you put up with this behavior, the worse his behavior will be. Why? Because you have unknowingly communicated to him you are a pushover. Perhaps one day, when you are tired of his asinine behavior, you blow up at him, which leads him to avoid *you*. So, why do we say yes when we really want to say no?

When we existed in tribes thousands of years ago, we *couldn't* say no for survival purposes. We worked together in packs to hunt and gather and fight off deadly predators. If you said no too many times, you would be kicked out of the tribe! This meant you would be exposed to the elements, as well as hungry beasts. Not to mention the risk of starvation—and say goodbye to finding a mate! Although we no longer have these limitations on our personal freedom, we still tend to have underlying beliefs around needing to please others, even to our own detriment. This is why boundary setting feels so awful, especially in the beginning. You have literally been neurologically wired to say yes.

Perhaps you are great at boundaries, but your partner is the people pleaser, as this is more common for women. If so, I hope the above information will help you support her in learning to say no. Hold tight. I will provide a list of ways to say no in a respectful manner within this chapter. Trust me, this will come in handy at some point in your life. We all need to say no at some point.

Men tend to have difficulty saying no in the work environment, which only perpetuates the imbalance in the emotional labor department at home. If you work long hours and are rarely home, who else will be managing the home, the kids, and the relationships in your life? This is another issue we need to address within our culture. We need to allow men to have a better work–life balance so they can better support their partners at home. As we have previously discussed, women are conditioned to put their needs last, so understanding boundaries for yourself is important. This will help you model that it's okay to have them and give her permission to have her own.

When boundaries are set and communicated clearly, our loved ones have guidelines on how to treat us. Communicating our boundaries with kindness and respect decreases the likelihood of conflict and hurt feelings. Although they may not realize it initially, they will eventually begin to notice how your relationship feels better. Below is the Boundary Bill of Rights created by Terri Cole, author of *Boundary Boss*. I highly recommend her book if you'd like to dive in deeper.

Boundary Boss Bill of Rights

- You have the right to say no (or yes) to others without feeling guilty.
- You have the right to make mistakes, to course correct, or to change your mind.
- You have the right to negotiate for your preferences, desires, and needs.
- You have the right to express and honor all your feelings if you so choose.
- You have the right to voice your opinion even if others disagree.
- You have the right to be treated with respect, consideration, and care.

- You have the right to determine who has the privilege of being in your life.
- You have the right to communicate your boundaries, limits, and deal-breakers.
- You have the right to prioritize your self-care without feeling selfish.
- You have the right to talk true, be seen, and live free (Cole, T., 2021).

Consequences of a Crossed Boundary:

If someone in your life crosses your boundaries, you will have to decide on an appropriate consequence. A *consequence* is a negative response that decreases the likelihood that the boundary crossing will occur again. When I say an appropriate consequence, I mean it's equal to the level of the transgression. If a neighbor borrows a tool and doesn't return it, the next time he asks to borrow something, you say no. If you think it's rude to say no, ask yourself who is the one being rude in this scenario. Your neighbor, who took your property with no consideration of whether or not you need it or how much it will cost to replace it! Maybe he is forgetful, maybe he's still using the tool, but perhaps saying no will prompt him to bring your property back and be better about returning things in a timely manner.

It is vital to respond to crossed boundaries with a consequence. Otherwise, the boundary crossers in your life will not take your boundaries seriously. They will think you don't really mean it. A consequence doesn't mean you make demands of the people in your life. A consequence is how *you* behave in response to the transgression. An example would be if you have a family member who has the habit of coming into town unexpectedly and demands a place to stay in your home. You would inform them they will need to ask at least a week in advance to ensure your guest bedroom is free. If they continue to show up on your doorstep without warning, you tell them they will be unable to stay with you. Perhaps you tell them where the closest hotel is and offer to drive them there. Sometimes, people cross boundaries because they are getting used to them or the new you. Sometimes, people may believe you are being unkind or selfish, but just remember, this isn't the case. It's because you care about the relationship that you are implementing these boundaries. It may take time for your loved ones to adjust, so you may need to be a little patient. People in our lives who want the best for us want us to have good boundaries. It's also a good idea to start small with loved ones. Making huge changes in a short amount of time may be overwhelming for some. However, if this boundary crosser is abusive, the boundary may be space. Physical, emotional, and mental space. Boundaries can be a gate, a window, a door, or a wall. It just depends on the situation.

There are seven types of boundaries I discuss with my clients. They are physical, time, financial, emotional, intellectual, material, and sexual. Let's examine each in order to begin to give you an idea of what *your* boundaries are.

Physical Boundaries:

This boundary involves your physical body. It may include how close someone can stand next to you. In some cultures, they stand closer, which can feel a bit threatening in our Western culture. Physical boundaries involve where you allow others to touch you and when. Are you okay with a hug when a friend greets you? Perhaps when you are fighting a cold, you keep your physical body away from others and request others do the same when sick.

Time Boundaries:

You can probably guess what the boundary encompasses: your personal time. If a friend continually runs late to planned get-togethers, you may decide to put a boundary in place with them. Perhaps a boss continues to call you on the weekend or after hours. This might require you to inform him you shut off your work phone after 5 p.m. and do not look at work emails outside of work hours.

Financial Boundaries:

This includes your personal boundaries around your money. You may decide you don't lend or borrow money from family and friends as a personal boundary. You may tell a friend at dinner you will pay for your own meal. You might say yes to the pet donation question when purchasing dog food. This also involves who you talk with about money. My husband comes from a family that does not talk openly about money unless necessary. Growing up in a low-income household, money was discussed openly and often in my home. This means Eric and I sometimes have different boundaries with money, so we have learned to compromise and respect each other's boundaries.

Emotional Boundaries:

Emotional boundaries involve allowing in emotions from others as well as sharing ours. If a friend calls you in the middle of the workday distraught, you may have to ask to get back to them after work. Otherwise, you know the conversation will upset and distract you. This could cause consequences at work and put your job at risk, potentially turning into a financial boundary crossing.

This is one I can speak to personally. When I work with clients, it is vital to have great emotional boundaries. I cannot allow my nervous system to take on my client's emotions, or I will burn out! I am a trauma clinician, which means I'm hearing the worst things that have happened to people 5-6 hours a day. I practice compassion, which allows me to empathize without fully feeling the impact of their emotions. Sometimes, I visualize a large stop sign when feeling overwhelmed or practice some somatic techniques to get negative emotions out of my body. Some clinicians utilize aromatherapy or crystals, but the best therapists address this regularly.

Intellectual Boundaries:

This means being allowed to share thoughts and opinions and allowing others to do the same. There may be situations where you choose not to share your beliefs, such as discussing politics or religion with someone who isn't open to hearing a different opinion. Intellectual boundaries involve allowing room to change our minds or time to consider or ponder an issue. This would also include being allowed to ask questions.

Sexual Boundaries:

Sexual boundaries include consent, timing of when a relationship involves sex, safe sexual practices, and privacy. They involve where we want to be touched, when we want to be touched, and what we need to feel safe. Sexual boundaries can include who we allow into our bedroom. We will discuss sexual boundaries in detail within the next chapter (Kathryn, 2023b).

How to Say No:

Say nothing at all. If you know someone will just argue with you and try to get you to back down, you don't need to communicate your boundaries. Some people will not be worth the breath it takes to explain. They haven't earned the explanation.

Don't offer an alternative option if you have no intention of following through. This will just cause confusion and give the person permission to continue to reach out.

- Thanks for asking, but I'm not available for…
- Unfortunately, that time won't work for me.
- I appreciate you asking me, but I cannot commit to that right now.
- I wish I could, but perhaps another time?
- No, thanks!
- Sounds like fun, but I already agreed to another commitment.
- I wish I could make that work.
- That's not my thing, but thanks for asking.
- I'll have to pass.
- I'd like to, but my body needs sleep.
- Thanks for thinking of me, but I'm not interested.

- Sadly, I already have plans.
- My priorities have to be with my family right now.
- Thanks, but I'm not taking on anything else right now.
- It's not a good time for me.
- Not tonight, but maybe next weekend?
- I'll have to take a rain check this time.
- I have allocated my spending for the year and will not be able to participate.
- This does not fall in line with my budget. I won't be able to help out financially.

How to Set Boundaries:

Remember, boundaries embody your personal values and morals. They are ways of setting limits so others will treat us the way we want to be treated. The first step of boundary setting is to figure out what yours are.

Take some time to think about your pet peeves. What bothers you? Is there someone in your life that continues to upset you? Write these experiences down and consider what boundary would be appropriate in response. Maybe your boss continually interrupts you when speaking. This may warrant a conversation about needing space and time to speak. I highly recommend using nonviolent communication when setting boundaries. Go back to Chapter 7 if you need to review the NVC formula. Always keep your side of the street clean. Be kind, courteous, and respectful when communicating boundaries. Unless you decide your boundary is no-contact, which obviously means you just remove yourself from this person's life.

If you run into someone you have cut out of your life, you do not even need to acknowledge them. If this snubbing doesn't fit in with your personal values, you can smile politely and walk the other way. Sometimes we put up with abusive behavior for fear of seeming rude, but it is important to protect our peace. If this person is harassing or stalking you, I recommend you reach out to law enforcement. Local domestic violence organizations will also be able to assist with going no-contact if you are having a difficult time. Technology has added extra windows and doors; if you aren't tech-savvy, you may need help closing these avenues.

Go through your values list and describe hard lines for you. For example, "I would never be rude to a server in a restaurant, and I always tip 20%." If you happen to have a terrible server who is extremely rude, this boundary may change. Perhaps you are civil but decide not to tip. Remember, sometimes boundaries can change depending on the situation.

Listen to your body. This may become your strongest alarm system. If something doesn't feel right in your body, it's important to get curious and listen. If you have chronic pain or health issues, this may be your body's way of telling you a boundary is being crossed.

Boundaries Are NOT:

- Nedra Glover Tawwab is a mental health clinician who has written books on boundaries and has been speaking about them for years through social media. In her workbook, *The Set Boundaries Workbook*, she explains boundaries are not:
- Pushing people to think or be like you.
- Managing areas of other people's lives that have nothing to do with you (mind your own business).
- Determining what others can or can't do with their lives.
- Demanding someone change for you.
- Manipulating someone into changing (Tawabb, N. 2021).

The Couple Bubble:

In the book *Wired For Love*, author Stan Tatkin explains the concept of the Couple Bubble. A couple bubble is a safe zone within which couples reside. The safe zone includes advocating for and being our partner's allies against hostile forces. The couple bubble would foster support, loyalty, safety, forgiveness, repair, accountability, appreciation, and connection. Dr. Tatkin also explains outside forces such as in-laws, addiction, and even children can disrupt the couple bubble. Our first priority is to our partner, which allows us to be a united front. Through supporting one another, we have the strength and energy to show up in the rest of our relationships in a healthy way (Tatkin, 2011).

Polyamory and the Couple Bubble:

Wired for Love doesn't go into details about the couple bubble and having an open marriage or participating in polyamory. If this is your current situation, work with a trained alternative sexualities therapist to help with appropriate boundaries. Polyamory means having an intimate relationship with more than one partner. There are several types of polyamory with different rules, hierarchies (or lack of), guidelines, and boundaries. This is not my area of expertise, and I hope to gain more knowledge and understanding throughout my career. All I want for my clients is to love and be loved. To have fulfilling safe sex (if they so desire it). Polyamory is gaining more attention, and more people are entering into these arrangements. Three years ago, I had not even heard the term.

Emily Nagoski, a renowned sex expert and sex researcher, explains in her book *Come Together*: "I want to say explicitly that polyamory can be beautiful, happy and life-affirming… and it isn't for everyone. Apart from the sheer calendar management of it all, it can be a big task, not to mention the time it takes to check in with everyone's feelings and make sure everyone stays clear about what's happening among everyone else" (Nagoski, 2024). A polyamorous client of mine once said, "Love is infinite, but time is not."

I believe we still have some work to do as clinicians to best support these clients. As our culture changes its definitions around intimate relationships, we will need to be ready to help clients navigate these changes in ways that feel right for them. The biggest challenge I see is a clash of values within a relationship. One partner wants to enter the poly lifestyle, and the other wants monogamy. I feel we have an ethical obligation as clinicians to avoid engaging in discussions on whether one arrangement is bad or good.

As I said at the beginning of our journey, any relationship can be healthy or toxic. Saying polyamory is bad or monogamy is bad is an oversimplification of the issue. What style of relationship you engage in should be in line with your personal values. I also feel we need to advocate for clients by allowing them to want what they want without attempting to change their partner's values. It is our role to stay curious and provide a safe place to explore. It's not my role to tell someone to betray themselves in order to avoid the pain and loss of a lost relationship. Some differences in values are too great to compromise on.

I think of this as being similar to when a partner decides they want a child and the other does not. How can we put a good or bad label on such a big decision? Such a big *personal* decision? If your partner is asking to change the arrangements of the relationship, remember your boundaries and values. They will help you stay on the path that is right for you. If you are open to exploring this change and it feels right for you (internally and externally), find an informed mental health expert to assist in this new journey. This will help you have a better chance of being successful. If you meet with a clinician and it doesn't feel right, try again. The process of finding a therapist who is a good fit can take time. My clients tell me horror stories of working with a therapist who just didn't jive with them. This clinician may be wonderful for other clients but not for them. I am the first to admit that I'm not the right therapist for everyone. It's just how it goes in the therapy world. Don't give up if you don't love the first one you meet.

Discomfort with Boundaries:

If setting and maintaining boundaries is difficult for you, I recommend you find support within your community. If you surround yourself with people who understand the importance of boundaries, you will be less likely to let yours slip. However, there are some cultures that encourage unquestionable loyalty to family or members of the group, such as older members. This is one area of struggle for some clients because this can result in taking bad advice or allowing others to take advantage of us. You will need to ask how to honor your cultural beliefs while maintaining what you need in order to take care of your mind, body, and soul. I don't believe any culture truly believes we should abuse one another. An interpretation of abuse as being part of a cultural belief is suspect. This balance of honoring one another while maintaining healthy boundaries can be tricky and confusing. If this is part of your personal journey, my heart is with you. I hope you are able to find a safe space to get to know and honor yourself.

NOTES :

CHAPTER 9:
Parenting In a Way that Just Feels Better (by Stephanie)

It's a Friday afternoon in the fall of 2023. My daughter Riley and I have just picked up her friend Ginny for a sleepover at our house. They are in the same fifth-grade class this year, and in true fifth-grade girl fashion, they immediately launch into talking about their classmates, singing along to the radio, and giggling while sharing funny videos and memes on their cell phones.

As I drive down the highway toward our neighborhood home in Beloit, Wisconsin, Ginny asks Riley, "Do you like your mom or your dad more?" I am, of course, interested to hear what Riley will answer, so I quietly wait for her response.

She pauses and seems to think for a moment before answering, "I don't know, my mom and dad are equally mean and nice," she says. I smile internally while keeping my focus on the road ahead. I am trying not to give away the fact that I have been eavesdropping on their conversation, but I am very happy. You see, this is exactly what I want as a parent—for my daughter to see my husband as equals in our parenting, a united front. *Parenting win*! I think to myself.

As a psychotherapist, I have had many individuals complain to me over the years that the main problem within their relationship is the difference in parenting styles. Parenting with another person can be difficult, but it is much more so if you have differing beliefs about how to parent. Major differences in parenting styles can not only cause conflict in your relationship but can also cause confusion for your child. This is because they cannot figure out how to meet the expectations of both parents when the adults are so divided in rules and expectations. This can lead to anxiety, depression, and even challenging behaviors.

Parenting Styles:

In the 1960s, psychologist Diana Baumrind identified and named the four main parenting styles: Authoritarian, Permissive, Authoritative, and Uninvolved. Authoritarian parents focus on maintaining control over their children with strict rules. They are also more likely to believe in using corporal punishment, such as spanking. Permissive parents often prioritize being their child's friend over parenting them and usually set very few rules, if any. Neglectful parents typically take on very little of the parenting role and usually do not bother to set rules at all. According to Psychology Today, "Authoritative parenting is widely understood as the preferred approach. Such parents are more pragmatic and flexible. They set clear boundaries but also encourage children's independence within those limits. Discipline in such families may be more supportive than punitive, and as children get older, their independence increases."

Now that you have a general understanding of the four parenting styles, you can ask yourself what category your own parents fit into and, if you have children of your own, which styles you and your partner rely on. If you are noticing that you and your partner are very different in your parenting styles or that you often disagree when it comes to rules and disciplining your child/children, this is a good time to consider taking a course in parenting *together* or seeing a couple's therapist who has a background in child and family therapy.

Realistic Expectations as a Parent:

Daniel Siegel, M.D., describes in his book *The Whole Brain Child* that a child's brain is like a house under construction because it is built from the bottom up. Dr. Siegel explains that skills like sound decision-making, control over emotions and body, self-understanding, empathy, and morality are created in the upstairs brain, or what we know as the middle prefrontal cortex.

"Just imagine the downstairs of a house that is complete and fully furnished, but when you look up at the second floor, you see that it is unfinished and littered with construction tools. You can even see patches of the sky where the roof hasn't been completed. That's your child's brain—a work in progress" (Siegel and Bryson, 2012). This means that you may have expectations of your child that they do not have the brain capacity or executive functioning to meet. Behavior can be a call for help when a child cannot meet your expectations. For example, if you tell your child to put their cell phone away and you later find them hiding with it in the closet, this is not a show of disrespect or defiance; it is them telling you they do not have the ability to put the phone away, and they need you to intervene.

As a parent, it is helpful to understand basic child development at each stage so you can have realistic expectations of your child as they grow. This is because a child's brain develops over time, and the skills they can master will depend on their age and their developmental stage. The exception, of course, being if your child is cognitively or developmentally delayed or impaired. Abuse and trauma can also stunt your child's development and growth, but we will get into that more in the next section. Below is a very simple breakdown of the five developmental stages healthcare providers use as a guideline for assessing a child's growth and development. For more detailed information on each stage, you can consult the CDC website: www.cdc.gov.

- **Birth to 2 months:** Can calm down when spoken to or picked up, smile when seeing your face. Can hold up head when on stomach, move both arms and legs, and open hands briefly.
- **2-4 months:** Looks at you, moves, or makes sounds to get or keep your attention. Makes sounds back when talked to. Holds head steady without support when you are holding him. Holds a toy when you put it in his hand. Uses his arm to swing at toys. Brings hands to mouth Pushes up onto elbows/forearms when on tummy.
- **4-6 months:** Knows familiar people, laughs, looks at self in mirror. Puts things in her mouth to explore them, reaches to grab a toy she wants, closes lips to show does not want more food. Rolls from tummy to back, pushes up with straight arms when on tummy, leans on hands to support herself when sitting.
- **6 months:** Fearful or shy around strangers, shows facial expressions that show emotion, cries or reaches for you when you leave. Looks for objects when dropped

out of sight (like his spoon or toy). Bangs two things together. Can get into a sitting position by themselves.

- **12 months:** Plays games, walks while leaning on furniture, drinks from cup without a lid. Picks things up with thumb and forefinger. Calls a parent "mama" or "dada" or another special name. Understands "no" (pauses briefly or stops when you say it).
- **18 months to 3 years:** Children can start playing pretend games, playing with other children, or following two-part directions. They may say the names of familiar people, throw balls, or run. Age 0-3 is when children begin to learn the concept of the difference between right and wrong.
- **3 to 5 years:** At this age, children start naming their likes and dislikes, learn to count to 10, and identify colors. They may recite nursery rhymes, know their name and address, and play on a playground on their own.
- **5 to 12 years:** In grade school, children grow their problem-solving skills and confidence. They may build close friendships, develop personal interests, and increase their reading skills. At ages 5-7, children begin to understand the concept of death and its permanence. Children do not understand the concept of respect or the use of sarcasm until age 5-6. The age of seven

has been considered the age where common sense and maturity start to kick in.

- **12 to 18 years:** Adolescents gain increasing levels of independence. They generally develop their own opinions, go through puberty, and become interested in dating and sexuality.

"Instead of raising children who turn out okay despite their childhood, let's raise children who turn out extraordinary because of their childhood."
– L.R. Knot

Medical providers today often use the Adverse Childhood Experiences Assessment (ACE) to determine the number of adverse experiences in childhood and their effects on the mental and physical health of their patients. We have included an example of the assessment below:

Prior to your 18th birthday:		
1. Did a parent or other adult in the household often or very often swear at you, insult you, put you down, or humiliate you or act in a way that made you afraid that you might be physically hurt?	No ☐	Yes, enter 1 ☐
2. Did a parent or other adult in the household often or very often push, grab, slap, or throw something at you or ever hit you so hard that you had marks or were injured?	No ☐	Yes, enter 1 ☐
3. Did an adult or person at least five years older than you ever touch or fondle you or have you touch his or her body in a sexual way or attempt or actually have oral, anal, or vaginal intercourse with you?	No ☐	Yes, enter 1 ☐
4. Did you often or very often feel that no one in your family loved you or thought you were important or special, or did your family not look out for each other, feel close to each other, or support each other?	No ☐	Yes, enter 1 ☐
5. Did you often or very often feel that you didn't have enough to eat, had to wear dirty clothes, and had no one to protect you, or were your parents too drunk or high to take care of you or take you to the doctor if you needed it?	No ☐	Yes, enter 1 ☐
6. Were your parents ever separated or divorced?	No ☐	Yes, enter 1 ☐
7. Was your mother or stepmother often or very often pushed, grabbed, or slapped, or did she have something thrown at her; was she sometimes, often, or very often kicked, bitten, hit with a fist, or hit with something hard or ever repeatedly hit over at least a few minutes or threatened with a gun or knife?	No ☐	Yes, enter 1 ☐
8. Did you live with anyone who was a problem drinker or alcoholic, or who used street drugs?	No ☐	Yes, enter 1 ☐
9. Was a household member depressed or mentally ill, or did a household member attempt suicide?	No ☐	Yes, enter 1 ☐
10. Did a household member go to prison?	No ☐	Yes, enter 1 ☐
To get your ACE score, add up your "yes" answers:		☐

If you are wondering what the difference between trauma and an adverse experience is, remember that trauma is anything that overwhelms the brain's ability to cope, which then results in the activation of the sympathetic nervous system (the fight-or-flight response). An adverse event can be something that causes someone great distress but does not always activate the sympathetic nervous system. Take a moment now to complete the ACE yourself. Then, think about how your parenting may be affected by the ways in which you were parented. Are there times when an injured past self is taking over when you respond to your child's behavior?

How does trauma affect the developing brain of a child? According to the National Child Traumatic Stress Network, chronic exposure to traumatic events, especially during a child's early years, can:

- adversely affect attention, memory, and cognition.
- reduce a child's ability to focus, organize, and process information.
- interfere with effective problem-solving and planning.

The Executive Functions that Trauma can Compromise:

- "Inhibitory control – the capacity to inhibit or regulate strong emotional or impulsive behavioral responses voluntarily.
- Cognitive flexibility – the ability to think about multiple concepts simultaneously or to switch quickly between concepts.

- Working memory – the ability to hold new information in the mind, process it, and store it as a learned memory."

From http://www.kappanonline.org/barr-trauma-hinders-learning/

The Long-Term Effects of Childhood Abuse and Trauma

There are common traits that I often see in my adult clients who have experienced childhood abuse and or trauma. Perhaps one of the most common of them is codependency. At its root, codependency is the inability to tolerate the negative emotions of the people around you. This results in putting the needs of others before your own, feeling personally responsible for solving others' problems, and feeling that self-worth is directly related to how much you can give or do for others. It can also be a lack of boundaries or the inability to say no.

Melanie Beattie, author of famed book *Codependent No More*, states, "Many of us codependents began to see ourselves as victims. Our painful history repeats itself. As caretakers, we allow people to victimize us, and we participate in our victimization by perpetually rescuing people. Rescuing or caretaking is not an act of love." Beattie also talks about codependency being an attempt to control others and situations.

When I identify codependency, I help clients set boundaries, say "no" more often, and self-regulate their emotions. We discuss prioritizing self-care and prepare for pushback from those who benefited from their lack of boundaries.

Discipline Vs. Guidance, Coaching, & Security

"There is absolutely no redeeming value in harshness. Harshness does nothing that loving kindness does not do better."
– Terrance Real "Us"

All parents must decide at some point how they respond to their children's problematic behaviors. Many of us respond by disciplining the way we were disciplined or what was modeled for us when we were children. An enormous amount of research has been conducted over the past several decades about common forms of aversive discipline and how they affect children. Aversive discipline uses techniques such as yelling or spanking.

Lucie Cluver, a professor of child and family social work at Oxford University, states, "The evidence is clear: shouting and hitting simply do not work and can do more harm than good in the long run. Repeated shouting and hitting can even adversely impact a child's entire life. The continued "toxic stress" it creates can lead to a host of negative outcomes like higher chances of school dropout, depression, drug use, suicide and heart disease." Claire McCarthy, MD, states, "Children who are spanked have a higher risk of aggressive behavior (which makes some sense, as spanking teaches children that in some circumstances hitting is okay), mental health problems, intimate partner violence, and substance abuse."

Take a moment now to think about how you were disciplined as a child. Focus not only on how it felt in a physical sense if you were hit or spanked but also on how it felt emotionally. I often say to clients, "To be a child is to feel powerless the majority of the time." Think about the many times children are told each day what to do, where to go, what to eat, "Stop talking and listen," don't touch that, "No, you can't," etc.

Stacy keeps a very small pair of infant shoes in her office. She pulls them out and has her clients hold them when they are feeling shame regarding childhood trauma. This reinforces how small and powerless they were at that time, which can be very impactful in their healing process and toward self-forgiveness. Often, we blame ourselves as children when our caregivers fail to meet our needs. Why? This is a way of feeling some level of control and safety. If, as a child, I blame myself, I can work harder to be a good kid vs. accepting I am in danger of not getting our basic needs met because I have an inadequate caregiver.

Children need guidance, boundaries, and knowing what is expected of them. They also need consistency, predictability, and routine. Even if there is no abuse or neglect but things at home are unpredictable for a child, this can have negative consequences. Dr. Bruce Perry states in his phenomenal book *What Happened to You?* that "even in the absence of major traumatic events, unpredictable stress and the lack of control that goes with it are enough to make our stress response systems sensitized, overactive and overly reactive" (p 61).

If you think it is too late to positively impact your child, take a deep breath and know that it is not. Dr. Jackie Kennedy, author of the wonderful parenting book *Good Inside*, states that "when parents are willing to change, when they are willing to repair and reflect together, non-defensively, about moments in the past that felt bad to kids, the child's brain can rewire" (Kennedy, 2022).

Good Inside also discusses the concept of what Dr. Kennedy calls "building connection capital." She states that "we can't change behavior until we build a connection." She talks about how children have an emotional bank account and that "when we really connect with a child, see their experience, allow for their feelings, and make an effort to understand what's going on for them, we build our capital" (Kennedy, 2022).

The next section of this chapter includes some of our favorite tools for helping parents parent from a positive parenting approach. Positive parenting includes the following components:

- Self-regulation, healing, and managing our triggers so we can be available to our children from a grounded place.
- Building a positive relationship with our child through caring, teaching, leading, communicating, meeting needs, providing consistency of care, as well as unconditional love.
- Respect for children's autonomy and independence. Allow children to make mistakes.
- Setting limits appropriate to age and development. Logical and natural consequences for difficult behaviors.
- Be responsive to their emotions, teach them about emotions and emotion regulation.
- Warmth, love, and affection. Praise their hard work and efforts.
- Being present with our children without distractions. This means listening and showing interest in your child (Goodwin, 2021). This does not always include teach-

ing or asking lots of questions about what your child is doing or thinking. Asking too many questions or giving guidance can pull a child out of play.

Parenting Tips and Tools

Don't Take It Personally:

It is crucial that you do not take your child's behavior personally because it's *NOT* personal. Behavior is often a child communicating a need for help. If you immediately go on the defense, you will miss what your child is trying to tell you, and more importantly, you will miss a teachable moment. Teachable moments are those instances where we can teach our child a skill. It's best to teach skills when a child is calm, so focus on this first.

Sometimes, the best approach is to simply model the behavior you would like to see. "Geez, I'm feeling a little overwhelmed. I think I'm going to need to sit down and take a few deep breaths." Then, proceed to do just that. Make sure your breathing is loud enough for your child to hear. Inflate your belly on the inhale and breathe out slowly. Do at least three rounds of this. You may also say, "I'm going to go into the kitchen for a few minutes to breathe. If you need me, I'll be happy to come give you a hug, but I can't sit this close when you are screaming. My ears hurt when you scream." I have purchased noise-canceling headphones for the purpose of sitting with my daughter while she's screaming. This lets her know I am there for her no matter how bad she's feeling. It can be pretty scary to see an adult freaking out when our kiddos are already feeling overwhelmed by their emotions.

Typical Problematic Behaviors:

We have described common challenging behaviors below to help you better understand and manage them in healthy ways:

Lying: There are many reasons children lie, but typically, it's not to manipulate you and show you disrespect. If a child is manipulative, it's typically because they have learned this behavior from an adult. They are probably not fully aware of what they are doing. Kids lie because the truth can be too scary to face or to tell. They can also lie because they are not developmentally in a stage where they understand with clarity the difference between the truth and make-believe. Lying can be the result of a rigid, authoritarian parenting style in which a child feels there is no room for self-expression or that their own needs and desires don't matter. Lying becomes a defense mechanism. For example, your child hides his report card and tells you he didn't get one because he knows a C in math will result in abuse. However, compulsive lying is when children cannot seem to help themselves and lie despite it being obvious they are doing so. They know they will get caught and expect the lies to cause problems in their lives. Treating this type of dishonesty would need to be facilitated by a professional mental health clinician with training in this area.

Hitting: Children often hit when their bodies feel unsafe. This is because the mental, physical, and emotional experiences they are having are too intense. The prefrontal cortex, or part of the brain that allows for logic and understanding of the consequences of actions, is extremely underdeveloped during childhood. They cannot think their way out of hitting when the impulse is there. The impulse shows up, and the response to not hit comes too late. Then we yell at them, further increasing unbearable emotions of guilt and shame. We need to intervene when a child is hitting others for safety reasons, but how we intervene is important. You can say firmly, "I will not allow you to hit me," and then physically block them from doing so by holding up your hands. You can gently pick your child up if they are small enough to do so and physically move them to a location where they will be separated from a sibling, friend, or pet.

Calling names: Children use name-calling because they recognize that words have power. They may not even know the meaning of the words, but they pick up on the effect that they have on others. This may be a way to show that they are feeling powerless and frustrated or that you did something to hurt them. You must set boundaries with what a child is allowed to say to you, but do not take name-calling personally. If this boundary is crossed, you can walk away and tell them you will not engage with them until the name-calling stops. You may encourage a child to apologize, but do not force them. A gentle reminder or modeling this by apologizing authentically to our children when appropriate is great.

Refusing food: Sometimes, kids struggle with the texture of different foods; this is very common in children with Autism. Their perceptions of bitterness or sweetness can be very different from those of adults. Rejection of unfamiliar foods is actually a biological design to prevent kids from eating everything they see, which can prevent illness or poisoning. If your child is exceptionally picky about food, please see your pediatrician for a referral to a nutritionist or occupational therapist.

Refusing to say thank you: Children do not start to grasp the concept of gratitude until at least 18 months of age. You should never force a child to say "thank you" but rather focus on the emotions they experience when given a gift. You can ask, "How does that make you feel?" You can model gratitude for them as well by often talking about what you are grateful for. You can explain how good it feels when someone does something kind for us or how good it feels to hear thank you. Forcing a kid to say thank you or apologize is a power struggle, and you will never really win. You may think you have won, but you have just bullied your child into compliance. How authentic can an apology or thanks be from a place of forced compliance? Have you ever been on the receiving end of a forced thank you? It doesn't feel great. You can apologize for your child or say thank you for your child until they are old enough to grasp these concepts and understand their importance.

Refusing to say sorry: Children are sometimes unable to say sorry because they do not have the brain power to put themselves in another person's shoes or to feel empathy/sympathy for them. Again, apologies should never be forced, but they can be encouraged and modeled for children.

Refusing to hug a relative: When you force a child to hug someone, you are telling them what to do with their body. Most adults don't like that, so why would your child? You are also modeling that the person who wants a hug is more important than your child. It is vital to teach children body autonomy, the ability to decide what they want to do with their body, and who is allowed to touch them, even when a grown-up is initiating touch. This is especially important because it can prevent children from thinking they have to accept abusive, inappropriate, or sexual touch from someone. You can model this by asking for hugs instead of taking them or stopping touch instantly when they say "stop." I did this with tickling when my daughter was little. It was a great "kill two birds with one stone" situation.

Riley enjoyed being tickled, but she also learned she was safe to say stop, and her request would be respected. She will have this expectation of others and be wary of those who don't respect this physical boundary.

Refusing to do chores: Let's be real here: No one *wants* to do chores. Children can find them to be boring and menial, and they usually have much more interesting ways to spend their time, like playing or creating. They may have to get help completing chores because we are asking them to do things outside their ability. They also may know it's easier if you do them. That's not disrespect; that's logic. Children should do chores, but shaming or getting angry about this does not help. You can say something like, "I am noticing that you are struggling to get your laundry put away. Can you tell me about that?" Give them a chance to explain, validate feelings, and help with barriers, but do not complete the chore yourself. This is a great opportunity to practice problem-solving. You could ask, "What do you think would help you get your laundry done?" Also, make sure you are giving chores that are age-appropriate for your child.

De-escalation Techniques:

When our kids are dysregulated or overwhelmed by big emotions, it is our job to remain calm and help them de-escalate. We have included the steps to de-escalate your child below:

Intervene Early: Notice the verbal and non-verbal warning signs that may communicate your child is escalating. They may be clenching fists, pacing, breathing quickly, stomping feet, and becoming tearful or argumentative.

Calm Yourself: Pause to breathe and ground yourself. Children are more likely to mirror our behavior and calmness. You can use slower, lower tones of voice. Also, it's always good to get on their level so you do not appear overbearing. Sit on the floor with them or take a seat. Try not to approach them from the front. This can feel aggressive.

Do Not Escalate the Situation: Avoid trying to reason with them or lecture them on their behavior or choices. This will only escalate your child. They are not capable of hearing this when escalated due to the way the brain functions during conflict. Your child is in full lizard brain and functioning from fight, flight, or freeze.

Give Personal Space if Needed: Some children need distance when they are dysregulated, and some want more closeness. Ask your child what they want or need, and respect their wishes if they are being safe.

Validate Feelings: You can say something like, "I know you are sad that you can't stay up late tonight, and it's so hard to stop your game and get ready for bed when you are having so much fun."

Give Choices: Children do better when they are given choices because they feel like they have some control over the situation. You can say something like, "Do you want to get in the bath or shower in five minutes?" Just make sure you always give choices that are acceptable to you.

Discuss: After a difficult interaction, when your child is calm, you can reflect on it together. You can say, "Boy, you were really sad about going to bed last night. I could tell that was very hard for you." Let them share their thoughts and feelings. You can ask if there is anything you can do next time that would help them in that situation.

Repair: Dr. Jackie Kennedy states that the parenting hack she gives to parents most is to "get good at repair." How do you repair after you lost your temper with your child? Kennedy recommends to "say you're sorry and share your reflections with your child—restating your memory of what happened, so your kid knows it wasn't all in his head—and then say what you wish you had done differently and what you plan to do differently now and in the future." Repair is crucial because it prevents your child from being alone with their feelings and prevents them from feeling shame. Make sure that you are calm and centered before you attempt repair. You can reflect back to the toolbox for self-calming techniques to use in order to accomplish this.

Adult Children: Parent and adult–child relationships have been quickly changing in the United States for the past two decades. Psychologist Joshua Coleman wrote in a 2010 article that "a recent study found that overall, parents in the U.S. report more conflict with their adult children than parents in other countries." He cites that the primary reason for this is "based on how the relationship makes the individuals within those relationships feel." This means that adult children today who do not feel good about their relationships with their parents are more likely to have conflict with them regarding this and even distance themselves from them.

"Going no-contact" is a term coined first on social media. It means cutting off all contact with a person or persons and is commonly associated with adult children choosing to no longer have contact with their parents. There are typically attempts to set boundaries with parents first, which is called "low contact." A study by Kristen Carr, Amanda Holman, and others showed that "the difference between the parent's perspective and that of the adult child is usually enormous. In a study of 898 unmatched parents and adult children, the researchers found that there was absolutely no agreement at all about what had caused the estrangement."

Carr et al. state, "While parents tended to focus on their children's objectionable relationships or sense of entitlement, adult children honed in on toxic treatment or feeling unloved and unaccepted. Interestingly, while the adult children were able to be explicit about why they felt unloved or unsupported and connected those feelings to their parents' behaviors, the parents showed very little self-reflection."

How do you avoid having your child or children cut you out of your life? Well, Jim Burns, author of the book *Doing Life With Your Adult Children; Keep Your Mouth Shut and The Welcome Mat Out,* talks about how your parenting role changes when your children become adults and likens this to having a new job description. Burns states that "the quicker you can embrace your new role, and, yes, even grieve the loss of your old role, the better it is for everyone." He describes this new role as being encouraging but not intrusive, being caring but not enabling dependency, and investing in your own health and well-being. Burns also discusses the importance of not giving unsolicited advice and becoming a student of their life. The parenting role is less about control, and adult children do not typically respond well to being told what to do. This can be a hard habit to break. Burns states, "If you want your adult kids to listen to you, you need to transition from being a controlling parent to being a mentor and coach."

In conclusion, parenting is tough, to say the least. The important takeaway from this chapter is that it is never too late to parent in a healthy way. Repair is crucial when you have mis-stepped or overacted to your child. The relationships between adult children and their parents are quickly changing within American culture. This requires that you change old ways of thinking and your role in their lives. Remember what we said about cognitive flexibility? This applies to parenting as well. We encourage you to work with a professional mental health clinician to get to know your inner self so you can heal in order to be the parent and partner you want to b

NOTES :

CHAPTER 10:

Let's Talk About Sex! (by Stacy)

Disclaimer: This chapter will discuss topics that may be difficult for some readers due to past sexual experiences. You may wish to read this chapter in small sections with breaks in between, or you may choose to put this chapter aside until you work with a trained mental health professional. If you feel overwhelmed by the material, please do what you need to do to take care of yourself.

One of my first graduate courses was an introduction to sex therapy. I remember the professor saying, "If you are going to work with people, sex will come up eventually. You will need to have some ability to discuss it openly and know how to help." I have never regretted taking this course. Sex is an important part of most romantic relationships, so I didn't feel this book would be complete without discussing it in some depth. We will not be able to discuss every issue exhaustively, but I will do my best to help you feel more knowledgeable and better equipped to deal with the most common issues couples struggle with in the bedroom. If your sexual issues are deeper due to sexual trauma, religious trauma, attachment issues, etc., this book will help you be better prepared to work with a Certified Sex Therapist (AASECT or ISTI).

This chapter will discuss erectile dysfunction, premature ejaculation, pornography usage, sexual consent, sexual boundaries, sexual dysfunction due to medical issues, sexual difficulties due to cultural, gender, or religious factors, as well as alternative sexual lifestyles and sexual abuse. This chapter also offers some resources that may be helpful to address the issues discussed. Let's begin by discussing typical sexual problems men and women experience.

Male Performance Issues and Sexual Dysfunctions:

Difficulty getting or maintaining an erection, premature ejaculation, low sexual desire, or difficulty with orgasm are common issues that can lead men to seek help through psychotherapy or seeing a medical doctor. These issues can derive from performance anxiety, but they can also be attributed to religious background, cultural beliefs, medical issues, sexual trauma, problematic pornography usage, or gender role expectations. I have discussed each of these aspects in detail below.

Medical Causes:

Some disorders, such as impotence, can be a side effect of medications. Selective Serotonin Reuptake Inhibitors (SSRIs) are medications often prescribed for anxiety and depression. Some common medications include Citalopram (Celexa), Escitalopram (Lexapro), Fluoxetine (Prozac), Fluvoxamine (Luvox), Paroxetine (Paxil), Sertraline (Zoloft), and Vortioxetine (Trintellix). Unfortunately, these medications can have adverse sexual side effects. Some side effects include impotency, low sexual desire, difficulty or inability to orgasm (Harvard Health, 2023). Other health issues, such as cancer, sexually transmitted diseases (STIs), heart disease, obesity, spinal cord injury, sleep disorders, Parkinson's disease, Multiple Sclerosis, tobacco use, alcohol use, and diabetes, have a higher risk for sexual dysfunction (*MSN*, n.d.). Erectile dysfunction can be caused by disruption in blood flow to the penis. Medications can be prescribed that relax the muscles in the penis and allow for more blood flow (*Erectile Dysfunction - Diagnosis and Treatment - Mayo Clinic*, 2022). Speak with your medical provider if you suspect your sexual difficulties have a medical cause.

A Performance of Two – Performance Anxiety:

Performance anxiety is experienced by most men to varying degrees at some point in their sexual lives. This involves difficulties with intercourse due to thoughts and worries over size of penis, stamina, hardness, as well as whether their partner is enjoying herself. Some men feel as if they must pretend to be someone else because their partner enjoys a degree of "rough" sex play. This may not be an issue for you personally, but for some men, this feels inauthentic and outside of their typical mood or manner. For some men, this leans too closely toward violence and can trigger fears of losing control. If you grew up in a home where violence was a common occurrence, you may feel uncomfortable approaching any behavior that reflects aggression, even in the sexual realm.

Performance fears can create the perfect recipe for disaster. Impotence or erectile dysfunction (ED), for example, can have biological causes but can also simply be due to *worrying* about impotence. A self-fulfilling prophecy, if you will. Sometimes, discussing this with your partner can help alleviate enough anxiety to resolve the issue. Practicing self-regulation skills, such as deep breathing or mindfulness, may also be effective. For sex to be enjoyable, we *must* be relaxed. You cannot orgasm when feeling high levels of anxiety. So, ask yourself, what helps you relax? How can you integrate this into your sex life? We will talk more about mindfulness below.

Premature Ejaculation:

Premature ejaculation (PE) is when a man ejaculates in under three minutes of sexual stimulation (this number changes depending on the source). PE can also greatly increase performance anxiety, creating a perfect catch-22 situation. Men ejaculate quickly because they are nervous, and they are nervous because they fear PE. Although the exact causes of PE are sometimes unknown, there are treatment approaches that can prove to be very effective. Before we dive into treatment, let's first examine some potential causes.

PE may be related to your first masturbation experiences. This may include frequent pornography usage. Frequent pornography use hasn't necessarily been defined, but some studies look at using pornography 1-3 hours a day. We will discuss both pornography and masturbation to determine whether one or both may be the culprit if you are experiencing PE.

There are many opinions out there in the mental health field on the value or harm of pornography. Like many issues, I don't believe pornography is *good* or *bad*. Again, there isn't a one-size-fits-all answer to this. Pornography can lead to problems within a relationship, or it can enhance your sexual experiences. Most therapists have a saying, "It depends," which is what I would say if someone asked if pornography is bad or good for a relationship. I feel it's important to discuss a few of these clinical opinions so you can make an informed decision about its use within your own relationship.

Pornography:

Pornography can create unrealistic expectations around sex for both partners. For example, it takes an average of eleven minutes for most men to climax during partnered sex (*MSN*, n.d.-b). In adult sex films, men seem to have never-ending stamina. These actors also tend to have a larger-than-average sized penis and can ejaculate to the ceiling. These images on screen can make you feel as if you are lacking sexual mojo. Due to common body image issues women have, knowing a partner is viewing films with women having perfect bodies can feel threatening. If you are viewing pornography and your partner deeply feels this is a level of cheating or betrayal, this *will* damage your relationship. Pornography use should be discussed openly with your partner and its use agreed upon. Pornography should not be hidden or lied about (for obvious reasons).

Some men enjoy utilizing pornography (alone) because this eliminates performance anxiety. There is no actual partner in the room to satisfy or perform for. There is no one to judge the size of your penis or how long you last. However, pornography usage can be linked to PE.

PE can become a neurological response to pornography. Typically, premature ejaculation is a habit created due to rushed masturbation. Daniel Sher, a clinical psychologist and sex therapy expert, states, "There are a few ways that masturbating with porn can indirectly lead to premature ejaculation. For starters, if a person rushes through the process, they may train their brain and body to ejaculate early, without even realizing that this is happening. This is a leading cause of PE. So, if you are masturbating in this way, you're putting yourself at risk. This is true whether you're masturbating with porn, or without it" (Sher, 2023).

Most adolescents begin masturbating with the need to hide and rush. No one wants a parent walking in when first exploring sexual pleasure! If you begin your sexual journey utilizing pornography, this can play a role in the need to hide and rush to orgasm. This is because of the stigma around pornography. Perhaps you come from a family where pornography was viewed as sinful. Some religious organizations believe viewing pornography is worse than murder! This would also encourage a person to hide and rush to orgasm if utilizing porn during masturbation. Fear of being shunned or punished can potentially create neural pathways in the brain, which tell your body to ejaculate quickly. Does this mean pornography causes PE? No, but it may put you at more risk for developing it.

Is Pornography Addictive?

The textbook used by mental health professionals to diagnose mental disorders, *The Diagnostic and Statistical Manual* (DSM-5), does not list pornography addiction. However, I have witnessed clients utilizing pornography in an addictive manner. This is not to say everyone who watches porn will become addicted, but I cannot deny that, for some, porn use is problematic. The World Health Organization classifies Problematic Pornography Use (PPU) under Compulsive Sexual Behavior Disorder (CSBD) in the International Classification of Diseases (ICD-11) but does not categorize it as an addiction. Recent research suggests that PPU aligns more closely with compulsive behavior rather than addiction (American Psychological Association, 2014). It seems for now, further research is needed but let's discuss what current research has discovered.

A cross-sectional study conducted in 2023 reviewed 66 articles on the determinants of PPU. The results of the study indicated that PPU had effects on the brain's systems involved in reward, cognition, reinforcement, and motivation. This means the brain's reward system is less sensitive and reactive over time with pornography use. The content of pornography, as well as the frequency of use, varied per study (Seyedzadeh et al., 2023). This change in dopamine functioning may lead to less joy in the bedroom, as well as a need for more extreme content within the pornography being used. A study by Cambridge University showed compulsive sexual behavior results in a need for more novel stimuli due to possible habituation (Banca et al., 2016). Seyedzadeh et al. also state, "Adolescents, who have been more commonly exposed to degrading/violent pornography, seem to be affiliated with risky behaviors. Particularly in females, such exposure is correlated with a background of victimization." Perhaps these risky scenarios being played out on screen may lead individuals to think violence and risk are acceptable or even normal. This is particularly risky for adolescents who are beginning to form their opinions around sex, as well as their sexual preferences.

Components of addiction include intolerance, withdrawal, risky behavior, consuming more than intended, continuous attempts to quit, cravings, inability to fulfill obligations at home or school, continuing to use despite negative responses from peers, engaging less in social activities, and, of course, an altered state of mind (McNeely & Adam, n.d.). All these components have been observed in my clients who report pornography addiction. I have had clients needing to view more and more taboo content each time to achieve orgasm. This is like needing more of a drug to get a "high" because there is now a level of tolerance built up over continuous, frequent use.

I have had clients bringing aggressive or hurtful behavior into the bedroom without the consent of a partner, knowing this would cause irreparable damage. This is like how individuals steal money from a family member for their next fix. They know they will probably be disowned or imprisoned if caught, but the craving is too intense, leading them to ignore the consequences of poor choices. This sexually harmful behavior my client reported was the reason he gave for his divorce. Another client of mine was arrested for voyeurism because this was the content of the pornography they were viewing. They knew it was wrong and against the law, which I think only intensified their arousal. The thrill of possibly getting away with it was too tempting.

Another client had a new baby at home and was putting his marriage on the line due to his pornography usage. His wife was supportive of his "recovery from pornography," but he knew if he "relapsed" enough times, she would leave him. Other people have reported financial hardship due to the cost of online subscriptions to adult content.

Although pornography addiction isn't listed in the DSM-5 as a mental health disorder, it sure can mirror one. This is enough of a reason for me to caution my clients. It may be perfectly harmless for you and your partner but watch for clues on how its use may be causing harm. If you suspect it may be causing difficulties, you may want to try cutting pornography out of your repertoire to see if it helps increase your sexual satisfaction in your relationship.

My personal concern about a large portion of pornographic films is that they tend to use plot lines where women are being coerced, manipulated, or objectified. I am not saying men who view this type of pornography will objectify or abuse women, but I do believe this will increase the likelihood for some men who are already prone to violence.

I also cannot help but argue these types of films support patriarchy. Again, is pornography bad? There isn't a simple answer to this question. There is no value in shaming people for using pornography, and this isn't my intent. However, if you are abusing your sexual partner in ways that reflect the pornography you have been viewing, shame might be an appropriate response. Shame might be a messenger informing you that this isn't acceptable behavior. Especially if you had to convince your partner to allow this behavior using control tactics. Go back to Chapter 9 for a review of boundaries and abuse. If abuse is present in your relationship, again, I highly encourage you to seek help from a professional who has training in working with intimate partner abuse.

Ethical Pornography:

There is now what is known as ethical pornography, which is easy to obtain. An article by monthly columnist, sex therapist, educator, and consultant Dr. Lexx Brown-James defines ethical pornography as including consent and diversity, with those involved in the making of the films being treated and paid ethically. These films embody multiple viewpoints, not just the typical male perspective and appetites (Banca et al., 2016).

Ana Bridges, PhD, a psychologist at the University of Arkansas, explains the difference between men and women with porn exposure observed in her studies. She states, "There can be a tendency (for men) to withdraw emotionally from the relationship. Those men report increased secrecy, less intimacy and more depression."

Ana further explains women tend to report more intimacy with pornography usage because they tend to use it *with* their partner. "Women, though, tend to watch couples' porn, with story lines and softer angles. When partners use porn together, they tend to watch things where both people are more egalitarian participants in a sexual act," Bridges says (Weir, n.d.).

Pornography can be an extra tool in your sex kit if both partners agree on how, what, and when to use it. For you personally, if your partner is adamantly against it, this may be a deal-breaker. I strongly discourage attempting to coerce or convince her. You will have to accept this as her personal value around the issue. This may be a fork in the road in your relationship. You will have to decide which road to take.

Treating PE:

The good news is that PE can often be addressed by utilizing mindfulness practices. Focusing on all your senses while having intercourse. Noticing the temperature of the room, the texture of the sheets, the smell of your partner's hair, the color of her eyes, and the sounds of your breathing. There is also the Stop–Start Method or Squeeze Technique.

Stop–Start Method & Squeeze Technique:

The window of no return is when sexual activity reaches a point when climax will happen if stimulation continues. Men with PE have poor awareness of when they have hit the window of no return, so ejaculation seems to come out of nowhere and often quickly.

The Stop–Start Method involves practicing stopping and starting sexual stimulation to prolong the amount of time before hitting the window of no return. You or your partner stimulates your penis until you are close to ejaculation. You would then stop until you no longer feel close to ejaculation (typically 30 seconds to a minute). It can help to take some slow, deep breaths. Repeat the Stop–Start Method three times, and on the fourth cycle, allow the climax to occur. Complete the Stop–Start Method once a day until you are able to increase time and control of orgasm.

The Squeeze Technique is the same as above, but instead of stopping all stimulation, one squeezes the tip of the penis (where the head meets the shaft) to decrease the level of erection. Hold until the urge to ejaculate passes. Make sure to stop or decrease pressure if pain is present (*How to Do the Squeeze Technique to Fight PE*, 2024).

Sex in the 21st Century:

I believe the sexual revolution we are currently in is both beautiful and problematic. Because we are exploring sexual identity, gender expression, consent, etc., there will be missteps. How we navigate, define, and express our sexuality and gender is truly an individual experience. This means we will have sexual likes and dislikes in common with our partners. We will also have things we enjoy that our partner does not. I see the most damage occurring when couples attempt to sway, manipulate, or coerce a partner into sexual activities they don't agree upon. For example, it is perfectly okay to want an open relationship or to engage in kink play if this fits in with your personal values around sex and commitment. If, however, you currently have a partner who is not interested in opening the relationship, don't shame them for feeling this way. We should avoid patterns of shaming individuals who want a more traditional monogamous relationship or want a form of "open relationship." Some individuals have no interest in sex, and this is also *perfectly* okay. Personal sexual exploration and expression should not require non-consent from a partner. It is important to respect a person's sexual boundaries, or you will damage trust, which will inevitably kill your sex life and relationship.

Throwing a Temper Tantrum for Sex:

When you hear the words *temper tantrum,* what comes to mind? I see a small, round baby on the ground, screaming and crying to get what he wants. This isn't because he's hurt or neglected; this is because he wants something he cannot have. This image is in no way sexy. Sexual desire is the last thing that comes to mind. When my clients describe a partner who pouts, gets passive-aggressive, says hurtful things, threatens to leave or find another sexual partner, or locks them out of the bedroom in response to saying no to sex, their partner is throwing a temper tantrum. I have heard different accounts over the years of this same scenario enough times to make my head spin. It's shocking how often partners think this approach will work. It's almost laughable because these behaviors do the opposite of what you are hoping to achieve. Your partner is less likely to want to get close when you are behaving in such a way. If they decide to give in and have sex with you to avoid the temper tantrum, you run the risk of more serious damage to your relationship.

In his awe-inspiring book *The New Rules of Marriage*, Terrence Real explains, "I have been amazed at how many partners—more often men—feel it is their right to be sexually serviced when they want to be…there's a place for saying, 'I'm not turned on this particular second, but I know if we get started, I'll get into it.' There's even a place for being generous sexually, as well as in every other way. But there's a difference between all of these and feeling coerced. I tell the men I work with that the price they will pay in the long run for not respecting sexual boundaries is the drying up of their mate's real desire for them- not infrequently to the point of their being thoroughly disgusted or repulsed by the partners they no longer give in to" (Real, 2007).

Vaginismus:

Vaginismus is a condition where the muscles of the vaginal wall spasm or contract when attempting to have intercourse or insert a tampon. This condition can be extremely painful (Dyspareunia) and can put a stop to all penetrative sex (Goodman, 2024). Sexual trauma can cause vaginismus and dyspareunia. There are treatments for this condition, including Kegel exercises or pelvic dilators (*What's Vaginismus and How Do I Know if I Have It?* 2023). I have had clients report symptoms of vaginismus in response to mistrust of a sexual partner or in response to sexual pressure from a partner. Keep this in mind before acting out when a female partner says no to sex.

Sexual Myths:

How Often Should We Be Having Sex?

Sex therapists often get asked how often one should be having sex. This is usually from the partner wanting more. There is no number for how much sex you should be having because it varies from couple to couple. Some partners enjoy sex several times a day, some once a month or once a year. If you are worried there is something wrong with your relationship, here are the criteria Dr. Tammy Nelson has described for a sexless relationship:

1. You're not having sex.
2. The thought of initiating sex makes you anxious or avoidant.
3. You never touch each other in a sensual way.

If you are in a sexless relationship, and this has been occurring for an extended period of time, you will most likely need the support of a sex therapist. Also, you might have a partner who does not value sex. This also doesn't mean there is something wrong with them (Nelson, 2022).

It's My Partner's Job to Please Me Sexually:

Some men have a belief their partner is responsible for their erections. This, again, has some cultural and religious roots. Unfortunately, this idea can directly feed into a woman's belief that part of her value is based on her ability to provide her partner with sex. Some women experience shame or depression when medical reasons impede their ability to have vaginal intercourse. Some women "host" men with their bodies to feel valuable despite having no desire to have sex. Studies show one of the primary reasons we have sex is because we enjoy seeing our partner's pleasure. However, if your partner's orgasm begins to feel like a job, your pleasure may become a burden.

All Sex Should End in Orgasm:

An orgasm should be viewed as a bonus to your sexual liaisons but not the primary goal. Why? Pressure to have an orgasm creates anxiety, which decreases pleasure, making orgasm less likely (DeSeta, 2021).

The Bigger the Penis, the Better the Sex:

The average male penis is 5-7 inches (erect). When women are asked about what they are looking for in an attractive mate, they rarely mention penis size. Women mention attractiveness, caring, kindness, listening, sense of humor, shared interest, and values. Penis size isn't important because sexual satisfaction for women is often about lubrication and clitoral stimulation. As discussed earlier, men are the ones who care about penis size because of what is typically shown in pornography. There is no current pill or procedure that can give you a permanently larger penis (Castleman, 2011). A larger-than-average-sized penis can be painful for your partner. The best advice is to learn to accept your penis as is and learn about lubrication as well as clitoral stimulation if you wish to be a great lover.

Intimacy Determines Ecstasy:

Esther Perell is a well-known sex expert and clinician. Her primary focus and study is on eroticism throughout the lifespan. She works with couples to repair their sex lives and support sexual vitality throughout the life of the relationship. Esther explains in her book, *Mating in Captivity*, "Love rests on two pillars: surrender and autonomy. Our need for togetherness exists alongside our need for separateness. One does not exist without the other. With too much distance, there can be no connection. But too much merging eradicates the separateness of two distinct individuals. Thus, separateness is a precondition for connection: this is the essential paradox of intimacy and sex" (Persell, 2007). This is because for eroticism to thrive, there must be some distance and mystery.

When we see our partners every day doing mundane things, our relationship can begin to feel like we are roommates or siblings. *Eww.* This does not mean you need to leave the country once a month, but this does mean that a healthy amount of space is good for your sex life. This is why having friends or hobbies outside of the relationship is important. We cannot expect our partner to always be all things. The clinical term for this type of fused relationship is called enmeshment. Ann Chanler, Ph.D, explains, "Enmeshed relationships are those that lack healthy psychological boundaries. We lose a sense of where we leave off and another begins. Our sense of individuality is compromised" (Chanler, 2014). So, when your partner asks to get a pedicure or go to yoga, remember this increases the chances of fueling her desire for you.

Sexual Non-concordance:

Sexual non-concordance occurs when an individual is physiologically aroused but not psychologically aroused. This means the body can show signs of wanting sex, but the mind does not agree. I am sure you have experienced an erection at some point in your life when sex was not even on your mind. The vagina produces lubrication for several different reasons, including sexual arousal, hormone fluctuation, birth control, sweat, or even infection (Cst-S, 2023). This can also go the opposite way, where your partner is feeling sexually aroused mentally, but their body isn't responding. This can be frustrating and embarrassing for both partners if they are unaware of sexual non-concordance. The best way to determine consent and desire is to ask. Don't assume lubrication is a yes to sex, or lack of wetness means your partner isn't into it. This is why KY jelly was invented!

Sex Should Happen Naturally and Easily:

Jimmy Knowles is a father, husband, and all-things-relationship enthusiast. With 1.7 million followers on Facebook, he provides content on how to be a loving partner and love the 21st-century woman. He explains in a video titled *How she experiences arousal and desire* there are different types of arousal and desire responses. Some people have a responsive desire, which includes a need for safety and emotional connection before they can feel aroused. Some of us experience spontaneous desire. Individuals with spontaneous desire are more easily aroused (*Facebook*, n.d.). This can be seeing your partner in the shower or watching a couple make out on TV. A small amount of sexual content is all some of us need to feel desire.

Gurit Birnbaum, PhD, Professor of Psychology and sex researcher, explains why foreplay begins outside the bedroom. Desire is dependent on whether your partner is responsive to your needs. This means putting your iPhone down, asking your partner about their day, and listening with interest. A responsive partner validates our feelings and truly cares about what is important to us (Birnbaum, 2023). Although Professor Birnbaum does a great job of explaining what a responsive partner provides, I also think we must include a partner who is a teammate. This means taking his/her share of the domestic and emotional labor load in the household. Being a teammate takes more than listening to and validating our partner.

A study reviewed in Medical News Today states, "Compared with men who reported making an unfair contribution to household chores, those who perceived a fair contribution to household chores engaged in more frequent sex with their partner, and both partners reported their sex being more satisfying" (Whiteman, 2015). I suspect this is because women feel supported by a partner who values equality and shows this by taking on household chores. Especially when a partner takes on the responsibility of grueling daily tasks, such as laundry or dishes.

Taking your fair share of domestic work also creates the possibility that your partner will have the mental capacity for sex. Many women have a constant to-do list running through their heads. If the sink is full of dishes, the application to summer camp needs to be completed, the planning of your next vacation or a visit from the in-laws must be done, sex will be the last thing on her mind. If you are unengaged with what goes on in the rest of the house, your partner will not engage with you in the bedroom.

When we are young adults and newly in a sexual relationship, arousal tends to come easily. Many of us assume it will always be this way. As we get older and have more responsibility—for example, kids and jobs—life can begin to feel overwhelming and mundane. This stress and boredom can easily trickle into the bedroom. As unsexy as it might seem, the longer we are in a relationship, the more our sex lives need more effort to thrive. This requires planning, including when, where, what will happen, and how you will make it happen. I highly encourage you to think of this time as a time to connect. This means not putting pressure on your partner to have sex with you.

Women Should Orgasm During Intercourse:

Most women don't orgasm during vaginal penetration and need manual stimulation of the clitoris. Only 21%-30% of women orgasm during intercourse (Spector, 2024). I have provided a diagram of the female genitalia below to ensure there is no confusion. No two vulvas are the same, but this diagram should help you with a basic understanding of where your partner might want to be stimulated. A good rule of thumb is to continue to have conversations about what she would like and when.

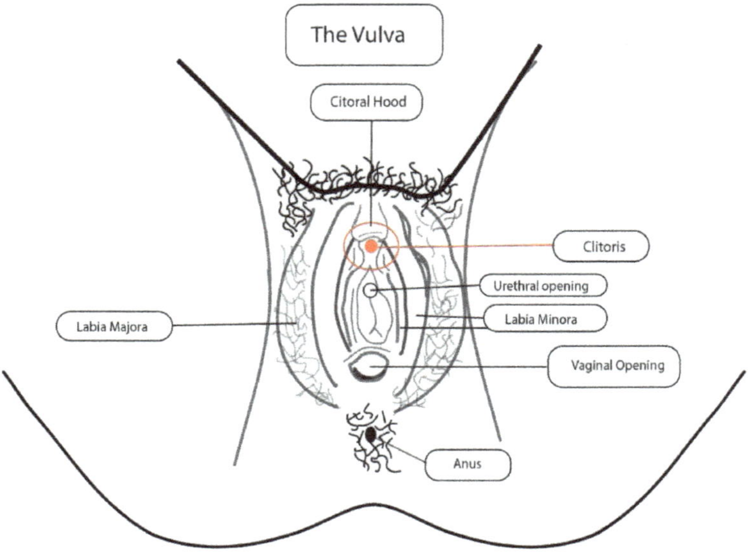

Religious and Cultural Factors:

Most religions have specific ideas and expectations about when sex is appropriate and with whom. Christian-based religions typically embody purity culture. This means spiritual worthiness is based on being pure or chaste. A common religious injury to our sexual exploration is sexual immaturity. Some individuals raised in devout religious homes were not allowed to speak about sex or ask questions. Some sex therapists must provide basic sex education and mechanics of sex to these clients. Sex can feel dirty or provoke feelings of shame due to purity culture messaging.

Gender Roles:

Brain imaging studies have shown heterosexual women respond to erotic images of women, couples, and even primates. These brain responses indicate sexual arousal; however, when asked, women did not report feeling sexually aroused. An article in Time Magazine studied 120 women over a five-year period. This qualitative study focused on sexual inequality or pleasure inequality. Most women reported cultural factors as the reason behind low desire or lack of interest in sex. This included previous sexual experiences where they were objectified, felt unsafe, focusing on their partner's pleasure, not feeling their pleasure was as important, feeling objectified, body image issues, having sex out of obligation, wanting to rush through the experience, as well as feeling numb (Rowland, 2020).

Why Do We Have Sex?

Sex is for fun, for pleasure, for connection, and (obviously) procreation. Sex should include an element of play where no one is taking things too seriously. It's a wonderful way to show someone love in a physical way, as well as connect on a deep level. Casual sex is what some people are looking for. Others may feel sex isn't for them unless there is an intimate connection. This connection may be more about just having fun, almost like sex is a sport. If there is clear communication around expectations, casual sex can work well for some. Unfortunately, within our culture, some people use sex to control others, to gain power, to cause harm, or to manipulate others. Some couples withhold sex to punish a partner. Some use sex as a bargaining chip ("If I have sex with you, will you watch the kid so I can spend time with my girlfriends?"). I don't know about you, but that feels way too transactional. Some individuals report sex can feel like a power struggle. Like quid quo pro, with a loser and a winner: "I did this for you, now you owe me." For some individuals, sex feels indulgent, such as having a slice of chocolate cake. Sexual urges and sexual acts can bring up feelings of being weak.

Then, there is obviously the worst form of these interactions, where sex is used to control someone through abuse. An abusive partner will cross sexual boundaries just to remind their partner they are in control. They may humiliate you by commenting on your body in hurtful ways. They may even refuse to stop touching you until you orgasm, which they feel alleviates any sexual infraction, even going so far as stating something like, "You obviously liked it." This is like saying, "S*he* said no, but her *body* said yes." Many victims feel intense shame for having an orgasm during their assault despite knowing the abuse would continue if they resisted. They may feel like their body betrayed them.

Alternative Sexual Practices: Kink, BDSM (bondage/discipline, domination/submission, sadism/masochism), & Sexual Fetishism.

Some clients engage in consensual and alternative sexual practices, including kink, BDSM, and fetishism. For the sake of simplicity, I will use the term "kink" to describe all forms of alternative sexual practices. Over the years, I have worked with clients participating in kink (kinksters), so I have made a point of learning more to better support them. This is not my area of expertise, and as I continue to learn more about this community, I realize there is still much to learn. I have attempted to cover a broad subject while considering this may not be relevant for most of my target audience of this book. I, however, felt it important to discuss alternative sexual practices to minimize harm and provide resources for those who may be curious or beginning to participate in this sexual lifestyle.

Most professionals and practitioners within the kink community would agree it is vital to learn safe ways to engage in this lifestyle before jumping in headfirst. Walk before you run; onset, clear communication, and aftercare are all parts of a successful "scene." A "scene" is a sexual experience where the participants have discussed in detail what will happen. The boundaries are clear, and safety has been prioritized. A scene may include role-playing, bondage, non-sexual touch, intense physical sensations, or inanimate objects (fetishism) (Tashra, 2023).

Individuals create a safe word, so, at any point, the play will stop if someone is feeling unsafe. This may be a need for a break, to change position, or to get a drink of water. If someone is unable to speak, participants come up with a hand signal or other way of signaling a needed halt in play. It is important to understand that consent can change from moment to moment, which is why a safe word or signal is a *must*.

Aftercare includes checking in with one another after the scene has ended. This allows couples to connect emotionally, mentally, and/or physically. Sometimes, individuals take this time to cuddle and speak words of love and kindness. They may choose to discuss what went well in the scene or what they would like to be different during the next. It is important to discuss with your partner what they need for their personal aftercare.

Consent to Non-Consent (CNC):

This is a form of kink where participants engage in "rape play." This involves someone in a dominant role and someone in a submissive role. Just like some individuals engage in thrill-seeking activities, such as skydiving or white-water rafting, rape play can be enticing for some, as it can provide an erotic adrenaline rush. Author and clinical psychologist

David J. Ley, PhD, states, [CNC is] "An extreme eroticization of powerlessness." (Ley, D., 2021).

A 2009 study by Bivona and Critelli found 62% of a sample size of 355 female undergraduate students reported having had a rape fantasy (Bivona, J. & Critelli, J. 2009). The best way to ensure these experiences do not cause harm is to choose a partner who is trustworthy.

The Sympathetic Nervous System and Kink:

As a trauma clinician, one of my primary areas of focus is the functioning of the Sympathetic Nervous System (SNS). We cannot turn off our sympathetic nervous system. The SNS will become highly activated if kink play involves feelings of being under extreme threat or danger. It is my understanding that scenes should not involve this level of SNS activation. Kinkster and Psychotherapist Laura A. Jacobs explains in an interview with Jera Brown of *Rebellious Magazine for Women* that kink has the potential for healing or harm. "Just because it can be healing doesn't mean it is healing. I suspect some people intuitively are drawn to it for those reasons and maybe intuitively enact it in those ways." Jacobs goes on to say repeating scenes like our traumatic experiences can result in magnifying the hurt; "If these scenes are replayed in a context of trust… the emotional meaning can be shifted from suffering to joy. Now those activities are about retaking control where one had before been powerless, feeling connection where one was previously isolated. Over time, the loving pathways can be reinforced" (Jacobs, 2021).

Traditional kink play involves exhaustive conversation around boundaries, expectations, and how to navigate the experience. In workshops and community spaces, we are warned: If someone doesn't offer to negotiate before a scene or if you get weird vibes from them, don't play with them. We're taught to use our voices and our intuition. As we explore best practices to make kinks healing and empowering, keep that in mind. It's not the kink; it's the way you go about it (Brown, 2021).

Some of the methods I use within my practice require dual awareness. This means my client must remember the trauma but not feel they are reliving the experience. They need to be aware they are in my office, safe, and not back in the traumatic event. One foot in the past and one foot in the present, so to speak. There is research on the concept of mastery for healing sexual trauma. This mastery involves repeating the sexual trauma with a safe and trusted partner to change the perception of the experience.

Author, founder, and director of The Center of Relationship and Sexual Health Joe Kort, PhD, states, "Trauma play is when someone learns how to "play" with their childhood traumas without putting themselves in danger or stunting emotional growth. A person learns to transcend his or her past rather than having it inflicted upon them. Using the example of the man who was physically beaten as a child, he may have some sexual kink in which he becomes physically aroused by being spanked or whipped. This is possible in a non-abusive relationship between consenting adults. Just as an artist may use past trauma to express herself in her work, a person may use past trauma to express herself in the bedroom. Nobody tries to get an artist to stop expressing past traumas!" (Kort, J., 2015). Although safety measures are in place, the research shows that people still get hurt. Consent boundary violations still happen. Dr. Ley also states, "Sex therapists and clinicians such as myself frequently encounter individuals whose information about how to engage in BDSM, CNC, or alternative sexual practices has come entirely from online sources, and contains a great deal of suspect and unhealthy information or practices" (Ley, D.J, 2021).

So, do your research and seek support from a professionally trained sex therapist operating with the best evidence-based practices. I will provide resources on kinks in the resource section at the end of this book.

Sexual Fantasy:

Dr. Tammy Nelson, Ph.D, sex therapist and author of *Getting the Sex You Want*, explains fantasy exists on a spectrum. This spectrum includes curiosity, fantasy, and erotic action. Sometimes, we fantasize about things we have no intention of acting out in our bedroom. We may be curious about things or partially fantasize about them. This could be certain actions, games, or having sex with other people (celebrities, friends, colleagues). What we do about our fantasies and sexual curiosity is called our erotic actions (Nelson, 2008).

Sex therapist Melinda DeSeta explains porn is fantasy. It is designed for pleasure and entertainment. It's not a "how to" video (2021). We just enjoy imagining it. We may wish to act out certain parts of the fantasy or attempt to play it out in its entirety. Just make sure consent and safety are at the top of the priority list when deciding on which erotic actions you will take.

Tools for Connection and Intimacy:

If you are currently experiencing sexual difficulties with your partner, most sex therapists will recommend a sex vacation at the beginning of treatment. This is so you can begin to build back connection and safety, which is fundamental for a healthy sexual relationship. If sex has begun to feel like an obligation, a job, or unsafe, you will need to first strengthen the foundation of your relationship. You will need to work with a sex therapist to determine whether a sex vacation is appropriate, as well as its recommended length. A sex vacation means no intercourse and no orgasm with your partner. This also requires you to take care of your sexual needs for a period. This is not permission for infidelity or the use of pornography if your partner isn't open to these options. Again, the nature of your relationship will need to be discussed and agreed upon. If you cannot reach an agreement or compromise, you will need to decide whether this is the right relationship for you.

The skills and tools below are ways of building safety through non-sexual connections. You may need to explain to your partner these are NOT for the purpose of getting sex from him/her. This is solely for the purpose of building back trust and safety. If sex occurs, think of it as a bonus, not an expectation.

Speak with Appreciation:

Dr. Tammy Nelson explains, "If you want your partner to do more of a behavior, express appreciation. For example, I love it when you go to the left instead of 'why don't you ever go to the left?'" (Nelson, 2008). Speaking with appreciation is a form of what behaviorists call Operant Conditioning. Behaviorism is a school of thought within psychology and is part of most clinicians' clinical repertoire.

Operant conditioning occurs when a learner's behavior is followed by a consequence or reinforcement. Positive reinforcement increases the frequency of the behavior when applied. If you tell your partner how much you love something, this is a form of positive reinforcement and will potentially increase the frequency of the behavior. It seems, most of us assume, that if we complain, we will get what we want, but the research says otherwise (Simply Psychology, 2024). Positive reinforcement feels better to give and receive, but it may take time to change old habits. Try writing a list of common complaints you tend to sling at your partner, and then, in a second column, write down something you appreciate about your partner in response to each complaint. Put a sticky note on your refrigerator that says, "Express appreciation," to remind yourself to move away from complaining to gratitude.

6-Second Kiss, 20-Second Hug:

Research has shown hugging someone you trust for 20 seconds or kissing for six seconds can release oxytocin, the love hormone. These extended hugs and kisses can lower blood pressure and heart rate, which tells your SNS you are safe. It might feel awkward at first, but after a while, you will notice your body relaxing into your partner's embrace (Nagoski, E. & Nagoski, A., 2020). Give it a try at least once a day!

Active Empathetic Listening:

Prominent psychologist Carl Rogers studied communication and refined this listening technique, described as Active Listening. The components of active listening are described below. This is a way of listening, communicating, and understanding, as well as encouraging the speaker to share more. The listener is an *active* participant, which is what most of us want in a listener (O'Bryan, 2024). We want to be understood and encouraged to share our experiences of this crazy world with someone who can be present. Active listening may be a great way to begin connecting with your partner if there has been a rift in intimacy. It's also a great tool for other aspects of your life, such as interacting with colleagues or friends.

- ***Show you are listening.*** Make eye contact, nod your head yes, show expression, smile, say things like, "Oh, that makes sense!" Make sure your phone is put away and the TV is off so you can be fully present with no distractions.
- ***Ask open-ended questions***. These are questions that do not ask for yes or no answers. Examples are: "Tell me more," "What do you think about…" "What did you do next?"
- ***Reflect on what you heard.*** For example, the speaker may say, "She didn't even listen to me, even though she asked for my opinion. She just nodded and then interrupted before I could finish my thought!" You would say something like: "If I'm understanding correctly, you felt unheard, and your opinion wasn't considered. Is that correct?"

- ***Avoid sharing your opinion or being judgmental until you feel you fully understand the situation (Viezzer, 2023).***

Dr. Amanda O'Bryan, in an article featured in Positive Psychology, explains, "In order to be successful in active listening, the listener must be authentic in their care. This reflects the principle of genuineness. Active listening can't be faked. Active listening requires true feelings of respect toward the individual speaking" (O'Bryan, 2024).

Sometimes, it's best to ask, "Do you want me to listen, or do you want me to try and help you solve the problem?" Sometimes, we assume our partner wants a solution when all they want is empathy. It's a good idea to get in the habit of asking.

Activities: Couples Who Play Together Stay Together

Find an activity you both enjoy and plan on engaging in this activity together at least once a week. This may be a date night in which you go bowling, food tasting, or ballroom dancing. Jamie C. Williamson, Ph.D, with the Huffington Post, explains there are three components of spending time with your partner that help the longevity of the relationship:

1. This helps avoid boredom. This also helps prevent the relationship from turning into a predictable routine.
2. The good feelings you experience during the activity will be likely to translate into the overall feelings of the relationship.
3. A fun activity tends to make us happy. When we are happy, we tend to extend this happiness toward our partner and the relationship (Williamson, 2017).

In Conclusion

The best sex is playful, with boundaries being respected. Sex isn't a weapon, a bargaining chip, a chore, or an obligation.

We hope your sexual journey is full of pleasure , joy and love.

Congratulations!

You made it to the end of the book! We knew you had it in you. Hopefully, this book has been more than just words on a page—it should be a catalyst for real change, deep reflection, and a push toward healthier relationships. But reading isn't enough. Healing and growth require action. So don't stop here—go find a therapist who challenges you, supports you, and helps you do the real work. You deserve it

Resources

This is by no means an exhaustive list but a few of our favorite resources.

Mental Health Resources

- **988** - A National Suicide Prevention & Crisis Hotline. Dial 988 for assistance | https://988lifeline.org
- **NAMI** | National Alliance on Mental Health | https://www.nami.org
- **DBSA** - Depression and Bipolar Support Alliance | https://www.dbsalliance.org
- **Tapping Solutions** | www.tappingsolutions.com
- **HeartMath** | www.hearthmath.com
- **National Domestic Violence Support** | Hotline: Call 1-800-799-SAFE | https://www.thehotline.org
- **Anger Management Courses**

- Framingham Massachusetts Anger Management Classes Online. Court Accepted Guaranteed Class
- **The Happiness Trap**: How to Stop Struggling and Start Living by Russ Harris
- **Self-Compassion**: Stop Beating Yourself Up And Leave Insecurity Behind by Kristin Neff
- **The Four Agreements**: A Practical Guide to Personal Freedom (A Toltec Wisdom Book) by Don Miguel Ruiz

Emotional Labor & The Mental Load

- **Fair Play** by Eve Rodsky
- **Fed Up** by Gemma Hartley

Men's Issues

- **I Don't Want to Talk About it** by Terrence Real, PhD
- **Boys and Men** by Richard V. Reeves
- **Facebook:**
  Jimmy on Relationships
  Zach Watson: #recoveringmanchild

Anxiety & OCD Support

- **International OCD Foundation | Obsessive Compulsive Disorder |** https://iocdf.org
- **D.A.R.E** by Barry McDonagh
- **Pure O** by Chad LeJeune PhD

Support for Couples

- **US** by Terrence Real
- **The New Rules of Marriage** by Terrence Real | https://terryreal.com | Terry Real | Creator of Relational Life Therapy
- **Mating in Captivit**y by Esther Perel | https://estherperel.com
- **Act With Love** by Russ Harris

Chronic Pain

- **The Way Out** by Alan Gordon and Alon Ziv | For managing symptoms of chronic neuroplastic pain
- **The U.S. Pain Foundation** | Education on chronic pain as well as support groups | https://www.bing.com/search?q=the+us+pain+foundation+&form=ANNTH1&refig=33ed3fe61e3047f2b8ec-8c880aa111d6&pc=U531

Sex & Intimacy

- **Come Together** by Emily Nagoski, PhD
- **Getting The Sex You Want** by Tammy Nelson, PhD
- **The Sexual Healing Journey** by Wendy Maltz

Trauma

- **What Happened to You?** By Dr. Bruce Perry & Oprah Winfrey
- **Waking the Tiger** by Peter Levine, PhD
- **EMDR Therapy |** www.emdria.org
- **Getting Past Your Past** by Francine Shapiro, PhD

Parenting

- **Good Inside** by Dr. Becky Kennedy
- **The Whole Brain Child** by Dr. Dan Siegal
- **The Explosive Child** by Ross W Greene, PhD
- **Trauma Proofing Your Kids** by Peter Levine PhD

Bibliography

Nelson, T. Ph.D. (2022). Pesi. Integrative Sex and Couples Certification Training. Pesi Publishing & Psychotherapy Networker. Slide 27, p. 9).

Goodwin, C., PhD. (2021, August 7). Psychology Today. *5 Evidence-Based Ways to Practice Positive Parenting. What is Positive Parenting and can it Really Improve Your Child's Behavior?* https://www.psychologytoday.com/us/blog/parenting-translator/202108/5-evidence-based-ways-practice-positive-parenting

Williamson, J. C., PhD. (2017, December 7). Couples who play together, stay together. *HuffPost*. https://www.huffpost.com/entry/post_b_12232928

Goodman, B., MA. (2024, May 4). *Vaginismus*. WebMD. https://www.webmd.com/women/vaginismus-causes-symptoms-treatments

What's vaginismus and how do I know if I have it? (2023, October 19). Planned Parenthood. https://www.plannedparenthood.org/blog/whats-vaginismus-and-how-do-i-know-if-i-have-it

Simply Psychology. (2024, February 2). *Operant Conditioning in Psychology: B.F. Skinner Theory*. https://www.simplypsychology.org/operant-conditioning.html

Viezzer, S. (2023, December 20). *Active Listening: Definition, Skills, & Benefits*. Simply Psychology. https://www.simplypsychology.org/active-listening-definition-skills-benefits.html

O'Bryan, A., PhD. (2024, May 24). *How to practice active listening: 16 Examples & techniques*. PositivePsychology.com. https://positivepsychology.com/active-listening-techniques/

DeSeta, M. Ph.D, (2021). Psychology Today: 5 Sex Myths That Keep You From Having Great Sex. https://www.psychologytoday.com/us/blog/the-modern-sex-therapist/202107/5-sex-myths-keep-you-having-great-sex

Castleman, M. (2011). Psychology Today: The Rare Truth About Penis Size: Are There Safe Effective Ways to Increase Penis Size? Yes.

https://www.psychologytoday.com/us/blog/all-about-sex/201101/the-rare-truth-about-penis-size#:~:text=Techniques%20to%20safely%20and%20effectively%20enlarge%20one%27s%20penis,lover%20%E2%80%94%20and%2095%25%20of%20penises%20are%20average-sized.

Spector, N. A. (2024, May 30). Why some women don't have orgasms. *HealthyWomen*. https://www.healthywomen.org/your-health/sexual-health/never-had-an-orgasm

Gurit Birnbaum, Ph.D, (2023). Psychology Today: Why Foreplay Begins Outside the Bedroom. An Emotionally Responsive Partner is a Powerful Turn-On. https://www.psychologytoday.com/us/blog/intimately-connected/202305/foreplay-begins-outside-the-bedroom?msockid=0965570811c66d543cd94255103d6c91 | Psychology Today

Ley, J.D., (2021). Psychology Today: Consensual Non-Consent: Exploring Challenging Boundaries. Exploring Complex Forms of Consent in Kinky Encounters.

Chanler, A. (2014). Psychology Today: Tangled Up in Enmeshment?: Using mindfulness to Lessen the Confusion of Fusion. https://www.psychologytoday.

com/us/blog/intimately-connected/202305/foreplay-begins-outside-the-bedroom?msockid=0965570811c66d543cd94255103d6c91 | Psychology Today

Whiteman, W., H. (2015, November 4). Men who do their fair share of housework have a better sex life. Medical News Today. https://www.medicalnewstoday.com/articles/301953#Sexual-satisfaction-improved-when-men-did-fair-share-of-chores

Nagoski, E. (2024). *Come Together: the science (and art!) of creating lasting sexual connections* [Book]. Ballantine Books. Pg. 92

Real, T. (2007). *The New Rules of Marriage: What You Need to Make Love Work*. Ballantine Books. Pg. 122

Perel, E. (2006). *Mating in Captivity: Unlocking Erotic Intelligence.* HarperCollins Publishers. Pg. 25

Facebook. (n.d.). https://www.facebook.com/reel/419974524175938

Facebook. (2024, May 9). https://www.facebook.com/reel/970351271014673

Ley, D. (2021). Psychology Today. Consensual Non-Consent: Exploring Challenging Boundaries. https://www.psychologytoday.com/us/blog/

women-who-stray/202102/consensual-non-consent-exploring-challenging-boundaries

Collier, L. (n.d.). *Growth after trauma*. https://www.apa.org. https://www.apa.org/monitor/2016/11/growth-trauma

Bivona, J. & Critelli, J. (2009). The nature of women's rape fantasies: an analysis of prevalence, frequency and contents. Journal of Sex Research, 46, 1, 33-45.

Harvard Health. (2023, July 7). Sexual side effects of SSRIs: Why it happens and what to do. https://www.health.harvard.edu/womens-health/when-an-ssri-medication-impacts-your-sex-life

MSN. (n.d.-b). https://www.msn.com/en-us/health/wellness/how-long-do-men-last-during-sex-here-is-what-the-research-says/ar-BB1oKlBy

Erectile dysfunction - Diagnosis and treatment - Mayo Clinic. (2022, March 29). https://www.mayoclinic.org/diseases-conditions/erectile-dysfunction/diagnosis-treatment/drc-20355782

MSN. (n.d.). https://www.msn.com/en-us/health/condition/in-erectile-dysfunction/in-erectile-dysfunction?source=bing_condition

Drescher, D., J. (2022, October). *What are Dissociative Disorders?* American Psychiatric Association.

Sex Abuse Healing - Healthy sex. (2022, April 8). Healthy Sex. https://healthysex.com/sex-abuse-healing/

Tashra. (2023, February 13). About TASHRA - Tashra. Tashra - Shaping the Future of Erotic Wellbeing. https://www.tashra.org/about-tashra/

Cst-S, J. B. P. L. (2023, February 14). You're so wet down there — what does that mean? Healthline. https://www.healthline.com/health/womens-health/vaginal-wetness#3.-Im-wet-down-there,-but-not-horny-what-does-that-mean?

How to do the squeeze technique to fight PE. (2024, March 4). Proactive Men's Medical. https://proactivemensmedical.com/blog/how-to-do-squeeze-technique-fight-premature-ejaculation/

Banca, P., Morris, L. S., Mitchell, S., Harrison, N. A., Potenza, M. N., & Voon, V. (2016). Novelty, conditioning and attentional bias to sexual rewards. Journal of Psychiatric Research, 72, 91–101. https://doi.org/10.1016/j.jpsychires.2015.10.017

Brown, J. (2021, April 8). BDSM for trauma survivors. Rebellious Magazine. https://rebelliousmagazine.com/just-the-tip-bdsm-for-trauma-survivors/

S.I., Seyedzadeg Dalooyi, H.A., Sharbaaf, M.S., Abdekhodaei, A.G., Chamanbad, (2023). Biopsychosocial Determinants of Problematic Pornography Use: A Systematic review. National Library of Medicine, v.15(3), 202–218. https://www.ncbi.nlm.nih.gov/pmc/articles/PMC10658102/

Zimbardo, P. & Ganus, M. (2016, March 1). Is Porn Good for Us or Bad for Us? New research suggests watching porn may lead to some undesirable consequences. Psychology Today. https://www.psychologytoday.com/us/blog/hero/201603/is-porn-good-us-or-bad-us

Rowland, K. (2020, January 31). I spent five years talking to women across the U.S. about pleasure and desire. Here's what I learned about inequality in the bedroom. TIME. https://time.com/5775442/sexual-relationships-inequality/

Sher, D., MA. (2023, May 24). *Does porn cause premature ejaculation? – psychologist explains*. Between Us Clinic - Sex Therapy Online Programs. https://www.

betweenusclinic.com/premature-ejaculation/does-porn-cause-premature-ejaculation/

Ishler, J. (2023, March 10). How to Release 'Emotional Baggage' and the Tension That Goes with It. Healthline. https://www.healthline.com/health/mind-body/how-to-release-emotional-baggage-and-the-tension-that-goes-with-it#Where-are-trapped-emotions-stored-in-the-body?

Tatkin, S. (2011). *Wire for Love: How Understanding Your Partner's Brain and Attachment Style can Help You Defuse Conflict and Build a Secure Relationship.* New Harbinger Publications. Pg 13, 136

Cole. T, (2021). *Boundary Boss: The Essential Guide to Talk True, Be Seen, and (Finally) Live Free.*

Kathryn. (2023, July 2). 15 Types of healthy boundaries and How to communicate Them - Center for Mindful Therapy. Center for Mindful Therapy. https://mindfulcenter.org/15-types-of-healthy-boundaries-and-how-to-communicate-them/

McNeely, J., & Adam, A. (n.d.). Table 3, DSM-5 Diagnostic Criteria for Diagnosing and Classifying Substance Use Disorders [abc] - Substance Use Screening and Risk Assessment in Adults - NCBI

Bookshelf. https://www.ncbi.nlm.nih.gov/books/NBK565474/table/nycgsubuse.tab9/

Weir, K. (n.d.). *Is pornography addictive?* https://www.apa.org. https://www.apa.org/monitor/2014/04/pornography

Yoga for Health: What the Science says. (n.d.). NCCIH. https://www.nccih.nih.gov/health/providers/digest/yoga-for-health-science

What consent looks like | Helping survivors of sexual assault and abuse. (2024, April 20). Helping Survivors. https://helpingsurvivors.org/what-is-consent/

Clara, H. Y.-. (2023, June 18). How is somatic movement different from yoga? - Hosh Yoga. *Hosh Yoga* -. https://www.hoshyoga.org/how-is-somatic-movement-different-from-yoga/#:~:text=In%20summary%2C%20while%20yoga%20and%20Somatic%20Movement%20share,asana%20performance%20and%20a%20set%20sequence%20of%20poses.

Sharma, A., Madaan, V., & Petty, F. D. (2006). Exercise for mental health. *Primary care companion to the Journal of clinical psychiatry*, *8*(2), 106. https://doi.org/10.4088/pcc.v08n0208a.

https://www.ncbi.nlm.nih.gov/pmc/articles/PMC1470658/

Self-Compassion. (2024, April 10). *Exploring the meaning of Self-Compassion and its importance*. https://self-compassion.org/what-is-self-compassion/#the-elements-of-self-compassion

Ruiz E. M, (2010). *The Four Agreements: A Practical Guide to Personal Freedom*. Amber-Allen Publishing.

Bastos, F. (2023, December 1). What are the 7 principles of mindfulness? The Core Tenets of mindfulness - MindOwl. *MindOwl*. https://mindowl.org/what-are-the-7-principles-of-mindfulness/

Bradberry T. & Greaves, J. (2009). *Emotional Intelligence 2.0. Talent Smart. Pg. 12, 24, 25*

Collis, V. a. P. B. R. (2022, February 19). *How to choose your values and why it matters*. Working With ACT. https://workingwithact.com/2021/12/27/how-to-choose-your-values-and-why-it-matter/

Hayes, S. C., & Smith, S. X. (2005). Get Out Of Your Mind & Into Your Life: The New Acceptance & Commitment Therapy. Oakland, CA, New Harbinger Publications

Trauma. (2024). In the Merriam-Webster Dictionary. https://www.merriam-webster.com/dictionary/trauma#did-you-know

Raikar, S. P. (2024, February 29). Limbic system | Description, Components, Function, History of Study, & Facts. Encyclopedia Britannica. https://www.britannica.com/science/limbic-system

Hynes, J., Turner, Z., & Transylvania University. (2020). Positive visualization and its effects on strength training. In Impulse: The Premier Undergraduate Neuroscience Journal. https://assets.pubpub.org/k9og4slt/31643844339559.pdf

Neuroplasticity. (2024, January 1). PubMed. https://pubmed.ncbi.nlm.nih.gov/32491743/

Kuo, J. R., Kaloupek, D. G., & Woodward, S. H. (2012). Amygdala volume in Combat-Exposed Veterans with and Without Posttraumatic Stress Disorder. *Archives of General Psychiatry*, *69*(10), 1080. https://doi.org/10.1001/archgenpsychiatry.2012.73

Chronic stress puts your health at risk. (2023, August 1). Mayo Clinic. https://www.mayoclinic.org/healthy-lifestyle/stress-management/in-depth/stress/art-20046037

Greene, P. (2022, July 2). *Your easy guide to DBT's TIPP skills (a.k.a. TIP skills)*. Manhattan Center for Cognitive Behavioral Therapy. https://www.manhattancbt.com/archives/1452/dbt-tipp-skills/#Temperature

WHERE SHOULD WE BEGIN? Season 6 episode 22 - You can be right, or you can be married. (n.d.). https://www.estherperel.com/podcasts/you-can-be-right-or-you-can-be-married

Romanelli, A., Weiss, A., Stone, J., Rettew, D., & Rettew, J., (March/April, 2023). Why Men Struggle With Their Emotions. *Psychology Today*, 28-33.

Coates, R. (2023, September 1). Opinion: White men have controlled women's reproductive rights throughout US history and the post-Dobbs era is no different. *Phys Org*. https://phys.org/news/2023-09-opinion-white-men-women-reproductive.html

Intimate partner Violence, Sexual violence, and stalking among men | Violence Prevention | Injury Center | CDC. (n.d.). https://www.cdc.gov/violenceprevention/intimatepartnerviolence/men-ipvsvandstalking.html

Kolbe, V., & Büttner, A. (2020). Domestic Violence against Men— Prevalence and risk factors. *Deutsches Ärzteblatt International*. https://www.ncbi.nlm.nih.gov/

pmc/articles/PMC7658679/#:~:text=The%20studies%20identified%20by%20the%20search%20yielded%20prevalence,reported%20having%20been%20abused%20or%20maltreated%20as%20children.

The Gottman Institute. (2019, August 26). *Marriage and Couples - Research | The Gottman Institute*. https://www.gottman.com/about/research/couples/

The Gottman Institute. (2024, March 5). *The Four Horsemen: The Antidotes*. https://www.gottman.com/blog/the-four-horsemen-the-antidotes/

Goldenberg, D., PhD. (2017, March 15). *Why men are resistant to therapy - PsychAlive*. PsychAlive. https://www.psychalive.org/why-men-resist-therapy/

Sullivan, E. (2016, July 13). *Self-actualization | Psychology, Maslow's Hierarchy & Human Potential*. Encyclopedia Britannica. https://www.britannica.com/science/self-actualization

Salzman, C. D. (2016, January 14). *Amygdala | Definition, Function, Location, & Facts*. Encyclopedia Britannica. https://www.britannica.com/science/amygdala

Šimić, G., Tkalčić, M., Vukić, V., Mulc, D., Španić, E., Šagud, M., Olucha-Bordonau, F. E., Vukšić,

M., & Hof, P. R. (2021). Understanding Emotions: Origins and roles of the amygdala. *Biomolecules*, *11*(6), 823. https://www.ncbi.nlm.nih.gov/pmc/articles/PMC8228195/

Dolan, E. W. (2024, March 3). Adherence to traditional gender roles linked to paradoxical sexual dynamics in relationships. *PsyPost - Psychology News*. https://www.psypost.org/adherence-to-traditional-gender-roles-linked-to-paradoxical-sexual-dynamics-in-relationships/

Cuncic, A., MA. (2021, June 22). *Amygdala hijack and the fight or flight response*. Verywell Mind. https://www.verywellmind.com/what-happens-during-an-amygdala-hijack-4165944

Harvard Health. (2020, July 6). *Understanding the stress response*. https://www.health.harvard.edu/staying-healthy/understanding-the-stress-response

Lee, S. (1965) *Amazing Fantasy #15* (J. Kirby, Illus. & S. Ditko (inker) Final issue. Marvel Comics.

Elderly white men afflicted by high suicide rates. (n.d.). PRB. https://www.prb.org/resources/elderly-white-men-afflicted-by-high-suicide-rates/

Madsen, R. W. D. E. S. D. M. C. a. D. S. R. (2021, October 26). *Utah Gender Wage Gap: A 2021 update*. USU. https://www.usu.edu/uwlp/blog/2021/utah-gender-wage-gap-2021-update#:~:text=Utah%20has%20one%20of%20the%20largest%20gender%20wage,disparities%20persist%20despite%20Utah%E2%80%99s%20comparatively%20strong%20middle%20class.

Piety and pay: Why religious states like Utah have larger gender wage gaps. (2021, January 8). *The Salt Lake Tribune*. https://www.sltrib.com/news/2021/01/07/piety-pay-why-religious/

Clinic, C. (2023, December 12). *What to know about older adults and suicide risk*. Cleveland Clinic. https://health.clevelandclinic.org/suicide-in-older-adults

APA PsycNet. (n.d.). https://psycnet.apa.org/record/2006-02929-013

Scottish Poetry Library. (2023, December 21). *The Guest House by Jalaluddin Rumi - Scottish Poetry Library*. https://www.scottishpoetrylibrary.org.uk/poem/guest-house/

Emotional numbness – PTSD UK. (n.d.). https://www.ptsduk.org/emotional-numbness/

B. Shaw. (2019, October 23). *When Trauma Gets Stuck in the Body.* Psychology Today. https://www.psychologytoday.com/us/blog/in-the-body/201910/when-trauma-gets-stuck n-the-body

Peter Levine on Trauma Healing: A Somatic Approach. (n.d.). https://www.psychotherapy.net/interview/interview-peter-levine

Pew Research Center. (2020a, August 17). *How Americans view gender equality as 19th Amendment turns 100 | Pew Research Center*. https://www.pewresearch.org/short-reads/2020/08/13/key-takeaways-on-americans-views-on-gender-equality-a-century-after-u-s-women-gained-the-right-to-vote/

It's 100 years since US women got the right to vote, but how has gender equality changed? (2020, September 1). World Economic Forum. https://www.weforum.org/agenda/2020/08/100-years-us-women-right-to-vote-gender-equality/

Cook, G. (2013, December 19). *Why We Are Wired to Connect*. Scientific American. https://www.scientificamerican.com/article/why-we-are-wired-to-connect/

Office of the Assistant Secretary for Health (OASH). (2023, May 3). New Surgeon General Advisory Raises Alarm about the Devastating Impact of the Epidemic of Loneliness and Isolation in the United States. *HHS.gov*. https://www.hhs.gov/about/news/2023/05/03/new-surgeon-general-advisory-raises-alarm-about-devastating-impact-epidemic-loneliness-isolation-united-states.html

Pew Research Center. (2020, August 21). *8 facts about love and marriage in America | Pew Research Center*. https://www.pewresearch.org/short-reads/2019/02/13/8-facts-about-love-and-marriage/

Lissak, G. (2018). Adverse physiological and psychological effects of screen time on children and adolescents: Literature review and case study. *Environmental Research*, *164*, 149–157. https://doi.org/10.1016/j.envres.2018.01.015

Nolen, J. L. (2024, January 9). *Learned helplessness | Description, History, & Applications*. Encyclopedia Britannica. https://www.britannica.com/science/learned-helplessness

Parker, G., Durante, K. M., Hill, S. E., & Haselton, M. G. (2022). Why women choose divorce: An evolutionary perspective. *Current Opinion in Psychology*, *43*, 300–306. https://doi.org/10.1016/j.copsyc.2021.07.020

Bieber, C., JD. (2023, August 15). Leading causes of divorce: 43% report lack of family support. *Forbes Advisor*. https://www.forbes.com/advisor/legal/divorce/common-causes-divorce/

DePaulo, B. (2018). Psychology Today. Why So Many Are Perfectly Happy to Stay Single. Put a Ring on it? All the Single Ladies Say: Not So Fast? https://www.psychologytoday.com/us/blog/living-single/201810/why-so-many-women-are-perfectly-happy-to-stay-single

R, J. (2024, January 16). *PRRI Census of American Religion | 2020*. PRRI | at the Intersection of Religion, Values, and Public Life. https://www.prri.org/research/2020-census-of-american-religion/

Wright, R. (2022, July 11). *Gospel Q&A: Should Latter-Day Saint women work outside the home?* LDS Daily. https://www.ldsdaily.com/personal-lds-blog/gospel-qa-should-latter-day-saint-women-work-outside-the-home/

From Esther Perel's blog - The 3 Types of Relationship Fights You Keep Having—And What To Do About

Them. (n.d.). https://www.estherperel.com/blog/the-relationship-fights-you-keep-having

From Esther Perel's Blog - Letters From Esther #36: Fighting with your Partner about Values? (n.d.). https://www.estherperel.com/blog/letters-from-esther-36-fighting-with-your-partner-about-values

10 most dangerous countries for women: U.S. is No. 10, according to Thomson Reuters Foundation. (2018, June 26). *CBS News*. https://www.cbsnews.com/news/us-10-most-dangerous-country-for-women-thompson-reuters-survey-amid-metoo/

Wright, R. (2022b, July 11). *Gospel Q&A: Should Latter-Day Saint women work outside the home?* LDS Daily. https://www.ldsdaily.com/personal-lds-blog/gospel-qa-should-latter-day-saint-women-work-outside-the-home/

Seariac, H. (2022, December 14). Utah religion: What's the religious demographic of Utah? - Deseret News. *Deseret News*. https://www.deseret.com/utah/2022/12/14/23507464/utah-religion-demographics

Introduction. (n.d.). https://www.churchofjesuschrist.org/study/scriptures/bofm/introduction?lang=eng

History of the organization of work | Industrial Revolution, Labor Unions & Automation. (1999, July 26). Encyclopedia Britannica. https://www.britannica.com/money/topic/history-of-work-organization-648000/Women-in-the-workforce

Theopedia. An Encyclopedia of Biblical Christianity. Complementarianism. (n.d.). https://www.theopedia.com/complementarianism

Nagoski, E. & Nagoski, A. (2019). Burnout: The Secret to Unlocking the Stress Cycle. Ballantine Books. Pg. 8, 16

Barr, B. (2020). *The Making of Biblical Womanhood: How the Subjugation of Women Became Gospel Truth*. Brazos Press. Pg. 17

Perry, B. & Winfrey, O. (2021) What Happened To You? : Conversations on Trauma Resilience, and Healing. Flatiron books. Pg. 258

Grossman, D. & Christensen, L. (2008) On Combat: The Psychology and Physiology of Deadly Conflict in War and Peace. Human Factor Research Group.

Infographics - Screen Time vs. Lean Time | DNPAO | CDC. (n.d.). https://www.cdc.gov/nccdphp/dnpao/multimedia/infographics/getmoving.html

The Danvers Statement - CBMW. (2023, July 10). CBMW. https://cbmw.org/about/danvers-statement

Wong, B. (2022, January 27). 'Weaponized incompetence' screws women over at work and in relationships. *HuffPost*. https://www.huffpost.com/entry/weaponized-incompetence-women_l_61e71983e4b0d8b665717814

Brown, A. (2023, June 23). 5 Key Findings about LGBTQ+ Americans. Pew Research Center. https://www.pewresearch.org/short-reads/2023/06/23/5-key-findings-about-lgbtq-americans/

Dust, F. (2020). *Making Conversation* (p. 22). Harper Collins.

Donner, F. (2020, February 12). The household work men and women do, and why. *The New York Times*. https://www.nytimes.com/2020/02/12/us/the-household-work-men-and-women-do-and-why.html

Thébaud, S., Kornrich, S., & Ruppanner, L. (2019b). Good housekeeping, Great Expectations: Gender and Housework Norms. *Sage Journals*, *50*(3), 1186–1214. https://doi.org/10.1177/0049124119852395

McRaven, W. (2017). *Make you Bed: Little Things That Can Change Your Life…And Maybe The World.* Grand Central Publishing. Pg. 9, 21

The role of Women in the Industrial Revolution | Tsongas Industrial History Center. (n.d.). UMass Lowell. https://www.uml.edu/tsongas/barilla-taylor/women-industrial-revolution.aspx

Tsongas Industrial History Center, Lowell, MA. (2015). *From farm to factory, the beginning of the industrial revolution in New England*. https://www.uml.edu/docs/Nutter_workday_FromFarmFactory_tcm18-203202.pdf

Hartley, G. (2018). *Fed up: Emotional Labor, Women, and the Way Forward*. HarperCollins. Pg. 189

Victorian Era. (2023, October 16). *Duties of Butler, Victorian Era Butlers, What is a Butler, Role Of Butlers*. https://victorian-era.org/duties-of-butler.html?expand_article=1

Brizendine, L. (2010). *The Male Brain.* Three Rivers Press. Pg. 80, 83

Pew Research Center. (2023, August 7). *Dads make up 18% of stay-at-home parents in the US | Pew Research Center*. https://www.pewresearch.org/short-reads/2023/08/03/almost-1-in-5-stay-at-home-parents-in-the-us-are-dads/

Thébaud, S., Kornrich, S., & Ruppanner, L. (2019c). Good housekeeping, great expectations: gender and housework norms. *Sociological Methods & Research*, *50*(3), 1186–1214. https://doi.org/10.1177/0049124119852395

Wanshel, E. (2023, June 22). Women call out men for using "Weaponized incompetence" to avoid household chores. *HuffPost*. https://www.huffpost.com/entry/women-men-chores-weaponized-incompetence_n_649483cfe4b007604cf797a1

Bologna, C. (2023, January 25). Small, actionable ways men can address unequal division of labor at home. *HuffPost*. https://www.huffpost.com/entry/how-men-can-address-unequal-division-labor_l_63cee556e4b01a436388cfc6

Gordon, A. (2020). Psychology Today. 4 Truths About the Division of Labor Among Couples: For labor division, perceptions, comparisons, and transitions matter. https://www.psychologytoday.com/us/blog/between-you-and-me/202005/4-truths-about-the-division-labor-among-couples

MensLine Australia. (2021, August 24). *Male stereotypes and the 'Man Box' | MensLine Australia*. https://mensline.org.au/mens-mental-health/male-stereotypes-and-the-man-box/

Romanelli, A. (2023). Psychology Today Magazine. Why Men Struggle with Their Emotions: Understanding the Push to Keep Feelings at Bay.

The Gottman Institute. (2022, August 25). *John & Julie Gottman - about | The Gottman Institute*. https://www.gottman.com/about/john-julie-gottman/

Rodsky, E. (2020). The Fair Play Deck: A Couple's Conversation Deck for Prioritizing What's Important. Clarkson Potter.

Rodsky, E. (2021). Fair Play: A Game Changing Solution for When You Have Too Much to Do (and More Life to Live). Penguin-Publishing Group.

Coleman, D. (2015). Traditional Masculinity as a Risk Factor for Suicidal Ideation: Cross-Sectional and Prospective Evidence from a Study of Young Adults. *Archives of Suicide Research*, *19*(3), 366–384. https://doi.org/10.1080/13811118.2014.957453

Greenwood, S. (2023a, March 1). *The Gender Wage Gap Endures in the U.S. | Pew Research Center*. Pew Research Center's Social & Demographic Trends Project. https://www.pewresearch.org/social-trends/2023/03/01/the-enduring-grip-of-the-gender-pay-gap/

Nash, C. J. (2009). Patriarchy. In *Elsevier eBooks* (pp. 102–107). https://doi.org/10.1016/b978-008044910-4.00982-2

Plank, L. (2019, September 14). Why the patriarchy is killing men. *Washington Post*. https://www.washingtonpost.com/outlook/why-the-patriarchy-is-killing-men/2019/09/12/2490fa7e-d3ea-11e9-86ac-0f250cc91758_story.html

Parenting Styles. (n.d.). Psychology Today. https://www.psychologytoday.com/us/basics/parenting/parenting-styles

Professional, C. C. M. (n.d.). *Child development*. Cleveland Clinic. https://my.clevelandclinic.org/health/articles/21559-child-development

How to discipline your child the smart and healthy way: Positive discipline for better mental health and physical health and a happy childhood. (n.d.). UNICEF Parenting. https://www.unicef.org/parenting/child-care/how-discipline-your-child-smart-and-healthy-way

McCarthy, C., MD. (2019, January 1). *The better way to discipline children*. Harvard Health. https://www.health.harvard.edu/blog/the-better-way-to-discipline-children-2019010115578

How Parents Can Start to Reconcile with Estranged Kids. (n.d.). Greater Good. https://greatergood.berkeley.edu/article/item/how_parents_can_start_to_reconcile_with_their_kids

Ehrenfeld,T,, (2021). Psychology Today. Childhood Trauma Shows Up in Brain Scans: Long-ago Trauma May Alter the Brain and Increase the Risk of Depression. https://www.psychologytoday.com/us/blog/open-gently/202106/childhood-trauma-shows-in-brain-scans

Streep, P. (2019). Psychology Today. 4 Things We have Learned About Adult Child-Parent Estrangement. Taking a Look at Contentious Topic Loaded with Societal Shame. https://www.psychologytoday.com/us/blog/tech-support/201911/4-things-weve-learned-about-adult-child-parent-estrangement

Fizyta, A. & Center for Nonviolent Communication. (2005). LIST OF UNIVERSAL NEEDS. In the Center *for Nonviolent Communication*. https://www.heartpsychotherapy.com/docs/NVC-NEEDS.pdf

International OCD Foundation. (2022, February 10). *International OCD Foundation | How do I stop thinking about this? What to do when you're stuck playing mental ping pong*. https://iocdf.org/expert-opinions/

how-do-i-stop-thinking-about-this-what-to-do-when-youre-stuck-playing-mental-ping-pong/

Sadurní Rodríguez, G. (2021). *Defusion: How to Detangle from Thoughts & Feelings*. Unknown. https://www.providence.org/-/media/project/psjh/providence/or/files/act-group-handouts/cognitive-defusion.pdf

Esther Perel. (2017, March 21). *Stop bickering. it's killing your relationship - Esther Perel* [Video]. YouTube. https://www.youtube.com/watch?v=xl7AcgjCyLU

Science and research. (2020, July 15). The Tapping Solution. https://www.thetappingsolution.com/science-research/

The science of HeartMath - HeartMath. (2024, November 6). HeartMath. https://www.heartmath.com/science/

What is ILF Neurofeedback? | The Neurofeedback Advocacy Project. (n.d.). Neurofeedback Advoca. https://www.neurofeedbackadvocacyproject.com/about-nfb

AdornThemes. (n.d.). *Science*. TheTouchPoint Solution™. https://thetouchpointsolution.com/pages/science

4 step thought blocking or thought stopping technique. (n.d.). Ann Silvers, MA. https://annsilvers.com/blogs/news/thought-blocking-thought-stopping-techniques?epik=

dj0yJnU9U2treW9ybEhpMlhXckZtSmhienRTS0NlS1UwaHhPR0MmcD0wJm49R29WT190cklaMlo5W1RYa3RKRG44QSZ0PUFBQUFBR2RUUkFz&utm_source=pinterest&utm_medium=social

Huffine, C. (1999). Twelve Reasons Why Couple's Counseling is Not Recommended When Domestic Violence is Present. In *Abuse Recovery Ministry & Services*. Abuse Recovery Ministry & Services. https://abuserecovery.org/wp-content/uploads/2018/05/Couples-Counseling-and-DV.pdf

American Psychological Association. (2014, April). *The perils of pornography*. *APA Monitor on Psychology*. https://www.apa.org/monitor/2014/04/pornography

www.ingramcontent.com/pod-product-compliance
Ingram Content Group UK Ltd.
Pitfield, Milton Keynes, MK11 3LW, UK
UKHW020905220925
8009UKWH00051B/998

9 798895 903742